SUSAN EASTWOOD

ISOLATED
WORLD

Growing up deaf in an uncomprehending society

SUSAN EASTWOOD

ISOLATED WORLD

Growing up deaf in an uncomprehending society

MEREO
Cirencester

Mereo Books

1A The Wool Market Dyer Street Cirencester Gloucestershire GL7 2PR
An imprint of Memoirs Publishing www.mereobooks.com

Isolated World: 978-1-86151-346-5

First published in Great Britain in 2014
by Mereo Books, an imprint of Memoirs Publishing

The address for Memoirs Publishing Group Limited can be found at
www.memoirspublishing.com

Cover design - Ray Lipscombe

The Memoirs Publishing Group Ltd Reg. No. 7834348

The Memoirs Publishing Group supports both The Forest Stewardship Council® (FSC®) and
the PEFC® leading international forest-certification organisations. Our books carrying both the
FSC label and the PEFC® and are printed on FSC®-certified paper. FSC® is the only
forest-certification scheme supported by the leading environmental organisations including
Greenpeace. Our paper procurement policy can be found at
www.memoirspublishing.com/environment

Typeset in 11/16pt Bembo
by Wiltshire Associates Publisher Services Ltd. Printed and bound in Great Britain by
Marston Book Services Ltd, Oxfordshire

Contents

Prologue

In conclusion

Appendix

Famous deaf people, and champions of the deaf

Prologue

You're in a supermarket and you see a man in a wheelchair trying to reach a packet of nuts on a shelf. Would you reach out for it and hand it to him?

You're standing at the bus stop waiting for the No. 12 bus, and next to you is a blind man asking you for the No. 63 bus. Would you read out the number and help him on?

A lady in a grocery store is struggling to put apples in a bag because she only has one arm. Would you offer her your help?

You're in a busy car park and you're annoyed because you're unable to find a parking space. Then you see an empty disability parking space. Would you park your car there?

Perhaps you would not hesitate – or would you? You can see for yourself what these people are trying to do - it's not invisible to you.

What are hidden disabilities? Let me name a few… autism, epilepsy, emphysema, mental illness, multiple sclerosis, arthritis, brain injury - or did you already know that?

Did I have to think long and hard about writing this book? The answer is, no. Perhaps it's best for me to leave you to learn for yourself.

Here are some questions about awareness.

How would you know? How would you recognise if someone is deaf?

Do you know the terms used to describe deaf people? What's the difference between 'partially hearing' and 'profoundly deaf?'

How many deaf people are there in the UK? The answer is 10 million – that's one in six of the population. Six million of them could benefit from a hearing aid, but only two million already have them. By 2031 there will be more than 14.5 million deaf people.

British Sign Language is:

- The first or preferred language for deaf people.

- Officially recognized by the government in 2003.

- A different language to English.

BSL is a visual-gestural language with its own vocabulary and grammar, and it's the preferred language for 70,000 deaf people in Britain.

Do you think we are being accepted in today's world, in the 21st century with the advances in theology and so-called awareness that is supposedly giving people a greater understanding? Then I'm afraid you are greatly mistaken!

Have I had it tough all my life? Judge for yourself.

In this changing world, life should be about principles, equality, respect, rights and dignity. My disabilities are hidden – does this mean I am not included within this world? Has society's attitude toward disabled people really improved over time? If only I could tell people about myself, would they understand when I really need help? Or maybe I should just explain why I am different?

If only it were that simple. For my part I don't feel as if I am within this 'equal' world, and I've felt trapped, frustrated, angry and all alone in this world for most of my life. How much has actually changed since I was born? It is hard to believe people that like me were once put in mental institutions for being 'retarded' or 'mentally ill'. Sometimes we were misdiagnosed by doctors - yes, it is true. Unfortunately, because I'm different, I have been called names like 'retarded' and 'monkey', and I even have been laughed at.

CHAPTER ONE

From 'The World Is Your Oyster' to 'Isolated World'

My mother borrowed a wedding dress and her sister-in-law's veil and married my father on June 30th 1956. Four months later, my father went into the Army and was based at Stratford-Upon-Avon. My mother went to live there for a while and when my father came out of the Army, they stayed at my grandmother's in Middlesbrough.

I was born in 1959 and we all stayed there for eleven months while my father saved up a deposit and bought our first home. We did not have much furniture, but we had the basic things, and that was enough for us.

My brother Stephen arrived in 1961, followed by David in 1962. We lived very close to the welfare clinic, which was about a five-minute walk from our house, and my mother used it frequently. I cannot remember our first home, but I have been told it was very large and stood opposite a primary school on a main road. Apparently I was always looking out of the windows and being very mischievous. At this point, my mother was expecting her fourth child.

One day when I was two years and ten months old, I went into the front room at the front of the house and climbed on to a chair, then up onto the table, to look out of the window. My mother then heard me screaming, and she ran in to find me on the wooden floor with blood streaming from my nose. I had two black eyes and a broken nose.

I was taken to hospital, where my parents were told there was nothing wrong with me. I had tape over my nose for a long time, as well as the black eyes. As far as my parents knew, no further damage had been done.

Some time after my accident, my mother took us to the welfare clinic. She explained to the doctor that my speech didn't seem to be improving, although I could count, dress myself and say nursery rhythms and I was toilet trained, could talk in sentences and could make myself understood. The doctor explained that he thought that my speech was not improving because I was jealous of my brother! My parents were then told that there was nothing to worry about.

But my mother knew something was not right with me – call it mother's intuition. If she called my name I would not take any notice. She took me to the welfare clinic again and the doctor quickly repeated that nothing was wrong. As time went on, my mother persisted at the clinic and she was told the same thing every time.

Then one day, she refused to move from the chair until I was given a proper examination. The doctor's idea of a proper examination was shaking a bunch of keys behind my head. He then declared I had hearing loss. When my parents were told I was deaf, my mother cried for a month and both my parents were devastated. The prospect of my being incurably deaf, to parents who didn't know what the future might bring for me, was soul destroying. They grasped every opportunity for help that was available. They soon discovered that there was practically none.

My mother took me to see a consultant, and I was given an ear mould. I had to wear a hearing aid, which was uncomfortable as there were two plastic pouches and two ear-moulds. It used one AA battery. I had to wear it over the chest with shoulder straps. Sometimes I would have it under my dress or in front of my top as I never liked it, but I was made to wear it all the time.

My parents asked the consultant a lot of questions, but the answers were not what they expected for the future of their child. The only help my parents got was from a social worker who came to the house and told my parents to make sure that I was facing them and to look at me every time they spoke to me, and they should speak to me slowly. She said I would have to learn to lip read. That social worker stayed for less than ten minutes to give that advice. When I think about that now, I wonder if she was even qualified for the job. I believe she had no idea that there was a language that deaf people used, or that there was a school for the deaf which used a different method of communication. Not a lot of help for my parents really. Has it changed for the better today? Please keep on reading – more about social workers later.

At the age of three my brother Stephen was told about my deafness. He was taught to learn to face me and speak slowly and tap me on my shoulders if he wanted my attention. I had to learn that and get used to it, as my parents did not know any other ways of communicating.

My parents knew nothing about the school for the deaf either, until I was three years and ten months old, when I was taken to a school in Orchard Road which looked like a big old Victorian house. When we arrived at that school, my parents witnessed something shocking. Why were the children and parents moving their arms about? My parents had never seen anything like it in their lives. They were using British Sign Language. Was I the only deaf child who communicated using speech? My parents didn't like it very much and they challenged the teachers about this 'language' they had never seen before.

It wasn't long before I picked up sign language and stopped speaking at home. I did not have to lip read at school! What could my parents do about it? Nothing, but they still had to take me to school because they did not have a choice at that time. I had to learn to use British Sign Language at school and lip read at home. I don't think I found it difficult because for me, I don't think I knew any different. I got used to it lip reading at home and using BSL at school.

I was there for a while, until I was about seven, and then I moved to a new school, Beverley School, which was newly built with huge fields and lots of classrooms and a big kitchen. This was very different from the one at Orchard Road. After a while I settled at Beverley School and the teacher had a word with my mother to say that I was doing very well and was above average compared to other deaf children in my class.

But my parents soon learned that my education was not at the highest standard, and felt that I was receiving a very poor education. They considered sending me to a better school, but how would they be able to do this? Not a lot of help was around at the time and Beverley School was not a Catholic school, although we were a Catholic family. My father was not Catholic, but he supported my mother's decision to give all of us a Catholic education. My father believed we all would get the best out of it, and wished for me to go to a better Catholic school.

I never wore school uniform while I was at Beverley. My mother made all my clothes and I always looked smart. My mother never went to work while we were children; she was a full-time mother. My father worked for British Steel and also did some handyman work on the side, so my parents could afford to take us all away on holidays.

When I was five years old, we moved to a lovely semi-detached house just round the corner from my grandmother's, with a nice garden and garage. I got the back bedroom and my brothers got the front bedroom with bunk beds. Some of our neighbours were friendly and we didn't live far from the park and the church.

From a very early age my mother spent a lot of time with me to help with my speech and education. She borrowed a machine from the school for a while, with headphones and a microphone. I would take off my hearing aids and put the headphones on and my mother would then speak into the microphone. I could not hear what was being said, but I could pick up the vibrations and tone of the sentence. I would then repeat the sentence she had just said. We would do this every night after tea and just before bed.

Mother also helped me to write and spell. Sometimes in the summer we did it in the garden and when we were finished, I would play with my brothers. I also went to dancing class for a while, which I enjoyed, and another partially-hearing girl from school came with me. I danced only to the vibrations I could feel through the floor.

In 1966 my sister Jill was born. I was seven years old and I remember coming home from school and there was my mother with a baby girl! I hadn't even known that my mother was pregnant. All I wanted to do was look after her. My brothers also used to help and teach me things - for example, I remember they used to ask me why it was important that we eat fish, and I would say because it had iron in it and things like that. We would sit around the table and have conversations and sometimes I was forgotten. When we were all at the table and I wanted pepper or salt, I would have to ask for it properly. I was not allowed to point with my fingers. I would have to say 'please pass the salt' - I was taught good manners. My parents wanted me to be treated just like everyone else in the family. There was no 'we feel sorry for her'.

I have always loved Christmas. I felt privileged because I used to get what I wanted - or so it seemed. It was the same for my brothers and sister. We got the same amount of presents from our parents, aunties, uncle and grandmothers, which made a lot of presents. I remember I loved my 'Tiny Tears' doll. My father used to film us opening the presents on Christmas morning. He even filmed the wallpaper in the living room, which had a horrible pattern of green leaves. One time I was given a typewriter, which I loved. I suppose it's one of the reasons why I wanted to work on a typewriter in an office. If my father had to work on Christmas Day, we would wait for him to arrive home at 2pm and then we had Christmas dinner together. I was allowed a tiny drop of beer mixed with lemonade.

I continued to go to school and signed with my friends, while when I was at home I would lip read. For me, that was normal. My parents were still not happy with the school, but the teachers continued to tell my parents that I was doing really well there.

When I was eight or nine years old my father suggested that I should walk to the bus stop and get the bus on my own to school. My mother was horrified and thought it was not a good idea, but I did go to school on my own. It was only about 10 minutes away. I remember walking to get the bus to school one morning when out of nowhere, a dog ran up to me and bit the back of my leg, for no reason. Whenever I see a West Highland White Terrier now, I hope it doesn't want to bite me! I have never like dogs ever since.

At Beverley School, we had a new headmaster and he had high hopes for us. I absolutely hated that school. I did not really like the other children and felt I was not learning anything. I never really made any friends at that school, though my family was still confident that I could do better in another school.

My father learned to drive and bought a car. Over the next few years my parents obtained brochures for St John's School at Boston Spa. The education, facilities and exam results there appeared to be excellent.

We attended mass every Sunday, and I would go to the Sister's house to learn religious lessons to prepare us for making our first holy communion. I went a few times with other girls, and had my first communion when I was nine years old, wearing a white dress my mother made me and a veil and white gloves. It was a lovely sunny day and we all marched along the route and then went into the church to make our first communion. Afterwards I had my photo taken in the back of the church garden. When I was at mass I would follow the service by reading the small book and my mother would point her finger underlining the words so that I could follow. I soon learned how to say 'Hail Mary' and 'Our Father' on the rosary beads off by heart. Sometimes, my brothers were altar boys at that church.

My mother saw Sister Vincent and spoke to her outside the church about my schooling. The nun knew of a very good school and advised them of a good Catholic school in York, which was the same school my parents had brochures for, Boston Spa. This meant I would be away from home, and my mother was not too sure about that.

My parents wanted to have a look around the school before making the decision about me going there. When we all visited the school for the first time we arrived at the front entrance of the building to see that it was a huge and very old building. From the front of the school, as you arrived, you had steps up to the front door. Inside was a huge hall with two parlours on both sides, and there was a church within the building.

The school was divided into two. One section of the school, on the ground floor, housed classrooms for hard-of-hearing children. The head nun, Sister Barbara, decided I would be on that side, as they said it was the best for my education. The other section of the school was for profoundly deaf children, and upstairs were the bedrooms, bathrooms, wash basins and toilets. We each had our own small wardrobe and curtain rails around the bed and we would have to close them at night (which reminded me of hospitals!) Those who were older had their own bedrooms, each with wash basins. I remember thinking it was nice to be able to have my own bedroom as I had always shared with my sister.

The area surrounding the school was beautiful and there was a nearby village and river. You could see fields for miles from the bedroom upstairs. It was lovely, especially when the sun was setting.

We went to the school for a look around and to meet the pupils. I remember having a walk outside the school, near the field, and seeing a girl with long ginger hair and a lot of freckles – we both smiled. My parents wanted to have a look round the other side of the school. When we visited the school for the second time this girl was in the classroom. I asked her for her name, and she said it was Joan. My parents spoke to the teachers again and the nuns told my parents that they had decided that I should be in the hard of hearing side of the school and believed it would be the best for my education. My parents were very impressed after having conversations with the teacher, and they decided I should attend.

In 1970, my parents got in touch with the education authorities and the head teacher of Beverley School to discuss me moving out of there to go to Boston Spa. After lengthy discussions, the head teacher visited my parents and said he would not try to stop me going to Boston Spa, as he knew my parents were all for my education. By then I was already wearing a new hearing aid which I could wear directly behind my ears (sometimes I suffered from it making a whistling noise).

CHAPTER TWO

A new school

I was 11 years old when I started at Boston Spa St John's School. It was a private boarding school and it took me quite a while to feel at home there. I didn't really enjoy staying there at first because I was away from my family. I had to lip read because we were not allowed to using British Sign Language, which was difficult sometimes. We would sign to each other when no teachers or nuns were around. Sometimes we got caught and we did get into trouble. The nuns even made a chart using star stickers, which was put on the wall along the corridor for everyone to see. It showed exactly who had been using sign language. The nuns would show everyone who had been caught doing the most stars. Despite these things, I do believe that my parents made the right decision, because I had not liked going to Beverley School.

When I first arrived at the school I couldn't wait to see Joan, as I felt I had a friend there. I did not cope well and was very homesick to start with. Being away from home and missing my brothers and baby sister was very difficult for me. I did receive letters from my brothers and parcels were sent to me with soap, sweets and letters. I have since found that the nuns would keep some parcels and not give them to me, because I would receive the most and the nuns were worried that other children would get upset.

Every other Friday I would be excited to pack my small case, for I was able to go home once every fortnight, but I was never happy to be returning to school on the Monday. At first I dreamed of going to another school where I could go home straight after school had finished for the day.

After I had been home for the weekend a few times, I got upset and threatened to run away. My mother told me not to be silly. My Auntie Joan drove us to school in her car (this was only the one time she took us – my father had to go to work that Sunday) and dropped me off at the school. When they had gone and Sister Catherine and I were walking down the corridor, she saw that I was still crying and slapped my face because I was upset that my parents had gone. I was in shock! It was Sunday teatime and she told me to go to the bedroom and get changed before meeting the girls in the living room.

When I went to get changed and put my clothes away, Sister Catherine was waiting. I said I would be all right and meet everyone in the living room, but then I quietly climbed out of the bedroom window and jumped down to the ground. I hurt my ankle and started limping. I kept on limping, because I really believed I would get home.

I kept on limping along until it was dark and I came to a house. I was lost, scared, injured and cold. I knocked on the door and asked the lady to call my parents and ask them to come and take me home. The lady kindly gave me some milk and sweets and said that she had called my parents. I hadn't given the lady my parents' name, so I was a little confused, but I was grateful that they were on their way. I was so happy! I remember looking at this huge real fireplace and felt nice and warm. It was a lovely bungalow and the man sat in an armchair smoking from his pipe. I couldn't believe I was going home!

I waited for about 15 minutes and then the lady went to answer the door. I was horrified to see Sister Catherine at the door with two police officers. She assured me that I had done the right thing by coming to this lady's house and asking her to ring the school. Again, I was confused by what she had said, but after what had happened throughout the day, I just went along with it.

I was put into the back of the police car, on the middle seat, with Sister Catherine at one side and a police officer on the other. When I got back to school, I was taken to the first aid room to have my ankle seen to. I found it painful to walk properly, so Sister Joan put cream around my ankle and massaged it. She was not so gentle, and she was disgusted with me for running away.

Then I was taken upstairs with Sister Catherine and another Sister. Sister Barbara was very angry. She came to me and said 'What will your parents say about all this?' while jabbing her finger firmly into my chest. I got more upset and said that I wanted to go home. I was taken to the bedroom, where all the girls were in bed. They had all been instructed not to talk to me, but Joan quietly climbed out of bed and came over to mine. She said that we should be 'pals'. I was confused and asked what it meant. She said 'friends forever' and we crossed our little fingers together.

A couple of days later my schoolmates were still not allowed to talk to me. On the Tuesday afternoon I was told to smarten myself up and was taken to the parlour room. I walked in and saw my parents! It was a shock to see them. They looked at me disappointedly, but not angrily. They told me that this school was the best for me and my education. They then asked the school for permission to take me for a walk down to the nearby village river, but they refused. My parents had made a 100-mile round trip and they had only been allowed to see me for five minutes! I remember that conversation as if it was yesterday.

My father continued to drive me to school once a fortnight. He would pick me up on the Friday and take me back Sunday teatime. Sometimes my brothers would come along to keep my father company.

It took me a while to get settled, but I did make some friends, particularly Joan. The school was very strict but it was a very good Catholic school. Boys and girls were kept apart most of the time and we could only see them during the lessons. What a very different world this was, and a very different way of schooling and educating, especially compared to Beverley School.

I started to enjoy going home for the weekend and returning to school. Sometimes I would have a friend come to my parents for the weekend. Joan came a few times and when she returned to school, she told everyone that my family was rich! We were far from rich, but my parents kept a very clean and tidy home. Another friend, Fiona, would come home with me sometimes too.

Every day we would have chores. Some of us would get up earlier to attend mass and then they would wake everyone up to have their beds made. When we were all ready, we would stand in a line until were told we could go for breakfast. Once we were finished, I would the clean the classrooms and sweep and tidy up. Some of us were given other chores to do. On Sundays we all attended mass, and we would follow it by using the projector in the church. A nun would use a big stick to underline each word so we could all follow the mass.

In the classrooms, the teachers did not use British Sign Language. They would speak to us by using a machine, the same machine my mother borrowed to help me with my speech. This was a waste of time, as I could not hear anything. The only reason I was in the Hard of Hearing section of the school was that my speech was quite good for someone who was profoundly deaf, and these machines weren't helping me at all.

Sometimes we would have nuns come into the classroom to teach us about religion. I must admit it was very interesting. I remember once Sister Barbara was telling us a story about Jesus and apostles. When she had finished, she asked if we wanted to ask any questions. I put my hand up and said, 'what does God look like?' Sister Barbara was not at all pleased and her response was 'Don't you ask me questions like that again!'

At lunchtime we would see the pupils from all sides of the school, and that was the only time we saw each other. When the school finished for the day, we would change out of our school uniforms and into our home clothes and return to our classrooms to do the homework which had been left by the teachers. After tea, we would go to the living room and relax by listening to music. At least, those who wore hearing aids and were hard of hearing could listen to music – I couldn't, but I could feel the vibrations through the floor, which meant I could dance to the beat. Otherwise we would watch television (without subtitles, as they didn't exist at the time). Sometimes, if we were all watching television, Sister Catherine (sometimes we would call her 'the house mother') would tell us what was being said and what the story was about and what everyone was saying. It was very difficult to follow at times, but it was the only way we could find out what was happening on the screen. The biggest problem was that if we were all enjoying watching a film and a man and woman were kissing, the television would be turned off! We would then have to wait a few minutes before it would be turned back on, as we were not allowed to see such things.

At weekends all the girls would go for a walk to the village and do a bit of shopping and spend time relaxing in each other's company. Times were changing in the way we wore our hearing aids. These devices fit in the outer ear bowl (called the concha). They were smaller and only fitted onto the bottom half of the external ear. I still hated wearing it, but I had to wear it whether I liked it or not during school.

Other times, during the day, if the head teacher or one of the nuns walked into the classroom, we all would stand up and say 'good morning', then sit down. We had the greatest respect for the teachers and the nuns. In school, I studied Geography, English, History, Maths, Biology, Art, Sewing, Cookery and Typing. My school report was always very good and my parents were always very pleased with it.

One time, in a biology lesson, Sister Maria decided to teach us about the differences between boys and girls. I really was excited, as I always wondered what 'it' looked like! She drew a picture, which was so simple I could not really see what it was. That was it! I was disappointed. We were never really taught anything that would go too far.

In my teenager years, I was mad about the pop singer David Cassidy. I was not a troublemaker at school. I behaved really well until one day, after school, I was doing my homework and a boy called Michael came into the classroom and asked me if he could kiss me, because he was leaving school! I quickly kissed him, but I did not really like it very much. I told Joan about it. That weekend, at teatime on Sunday, we were all in the living room when suddenly Sister Catherine came in and said to me straight away 'I want to have a word with you now'. I could not understand why or what I was supposed to have done wrong. We went into the hearing aid room and sat down.

'Do you have any idea why I wanted to speak to you?' said Sister Catherine. I thought it must be about me kissing this boy, so I said 'I have no idea'. She then said, 'Do you realise that you must think of your parents, and that they are the best parents in the school? Are you sure you don't know why I need to see you to discuss what you may have done?

'Yes' I said. I did not know what to say to that. She told me to go back to the living room and told Joan to come too. When Joan returned we were unable to discuss what had happened until we were ready to go to bed, which was always at ten o'clock when the light was turned off.

Joan and I quickly talked about what had happen in the hearing room. Luckily for me, Joan had told Sister Catherine that I had done nothing, but another girl, Agnes, came to me and said, 'It's was me that told Sister Catherine about you.' I quickly ran to Joan and told her about it.

Another time, one Sunday afternoon, an ex-pupil came to the school and wanted us all to go to the gym to show us slides of mountains, trees, rivers... yawn! I said to Joan that we would miss *Black Beauty*, our favourite television programme, so Joan told me to ask Sister Catherine for permission to allow us to go and watch it. 'Why me', I asked? 'Well,' said Joan, 'you are sitting next to her!'

I didn't really want to ask, but I did really want to see *Black Beauty* rather than the boring old slides, so I said 'Excuse me please, can we leave to watch *Black Beauty* in five minutes?' She said yes, or at least I thought she did. Brilliant I thought, and told Joan to come with me . We sneaked out quietly with another girl and ran laughing down the corridor, but just as we were about to go into the living room Sister Catherine came up to us in a rage and tried to slap my face. I put my arm across my face to protect myself. I remembered that she had slapped my face when I was upset over missing my family when I returned to school. Sister Catherine then raised her hand to Joan, but she too lifted her arm and the blow missed her face.

She told us all to go upstairs to our bedrooms and stay there – we never got to see *Black Beauty*. Joan and I were sure Agnes had told Sister Catherine about us. After everyone had finished watching the most boring pictures, Sister Catherine came to the bedroom and waited for us to apologize, but I really thought she had said it was fine for us to watch the television.

I made sure I would not get into trouble again. I never liked getting in trouble and never kissed another boy again either while I was at school. Joan smoked in the toilet at one time, which I never knew about. She too got into trouble for that when again, Agnes caught Joan and told Sister Barbara. Joan and I called Agnes the 'troublemaker'. Joan's ex-boyfriend had sent her the cigarettes, which I was surprised about. Sister Barbara sent a letter to Joan's parents to let them know about Joan smoking.

To help us prepare for our CSE exams, we would go and do work experience during school time by travelling on the bus. This was preparing us to face the world when leaving school. I worked at a few different jobs when trying to gain experience. One was at a small shop filling shelves with tins for about two hours for one day a week (it was the most boring job in the world!) and I did waitress service at a motorway café called Wetherby Turnpike Grill, which I attended six times. I received two reports for both jobs I did from both managers with the questions given, and the answers were the following:

'How well has she done the them?' Answer, 'Well'.

'Does she show any special aptitude for these jobs or any part of them?' 'Yes'.

'Communication: Do you find It hard to understand Susan's speech?' Answer 'Yes'.

'Does she find it hard to understand you?' 'No'.

'Have you come across any particular communication problems?' 'Yes'.

'In general, how you would describe Susan's personality?' 'Cheerful, pleasant.'

'How would you describe her application to work?' 'Industrious'.

'Would you be prepared to employ her on a full-time basis, for example does she compare favourably with the other employees or trainees you have?' Answer 'yes, in this particular capacity.'

'Have you noticed any special hazards arising from deafness?' 'No'.

This report was given to Sister Josephine, the Career Teacher. I also got another report from John Smiths Tadcaster Brewery Limited, where I did general office duties. The work was copy-typing and photocopying. How well had I done them? Reply was 'very well. A little more experience reading other people's handwriting would have enabled her to carry out copy typing more efficiently.'

'Does she show any special aptitude for these jobs or any part of them?' Answer: 'no outstanding aptitude but she seemed keenly interested in everything she was asked to do and would develop into a good copy typist'.

Communication: 'Do you find it hard to understand Susan's speech?' Answer 'no'.

'Does Susan find it hard to understand you?' 'No'.

'Have you come across any particular communication problems?' Answer 'No'.

General questions: 'How would you describe Susan's personality?' 'Calm, pleasant young lady, able to get along with other young people'.

'How would you describe her application to work?' 'Good'.

'Would you be prepared to employ her on a full-time basis, for example does she compare favourably with other employees or trainees you have?' Answer 'yes'.

'Have you noticed any special hazards arising from deafness?' Answer 'The tendency to exclude from normal day to day conversation when in a group situation'.

So working in the café was mainly cleaning the tables and putting plate pots into the kitchen. I didn't enjoy that either! The only perk was that I got a free lunch. I did very much enjoy working in an office half a morning doing some copying and typing. I did that six times. The money I earned was given to the school; I didn't keep it for myself.

During my time at school I was always looking forward to summer holidays, as we always went away for two weeks every year. We would go to different parts of the country, places like Bournemouth, Plymouth and Great Yarmouth; we did go to see a show once in which Lulu was performing. I couldn't wait to return to school to tell everyone about that! We also went to Stratford-upon-Avon, to a place called Eastbound, and we stayed in a caravan and I loved it. We would have our breakfast in the caravan and then go out for the day. We would return for tea, and then we would go to the fair or zoo, or of course the seaside and go swimming in the ocean. We would do various activities every day for two whole weeks. Every year we would have a different caravan. One time, we had one overlooking the river and a small bridge. It was beautiful and I always played with my brothers and sister. I remember all of us in the car when we were travelling. We would play 'I spy with my little eye'. Even sometimes at the weekend, if my father was off work, we would go to Stewart Park for a picnic.

I didn't really know what I wanted to do when I left school. The teacher, Miss Faye, asked me what I would like to do for work and I told her that I would like to be a catwalk and fashion model. 'Really?' she said, 'I don't think it's a very good idea, as you would have to go naked to pose for photographs.' I decided straight away that was a no. I thought no man was supposed to see your body until your wedding night!

After the summer holidays had finished, I would look forward to returning to school to see my best friend Joan and a few others too. That was my life at school and during my teenage years.

Eventually, the time came for all of us to leave school. It was sad and I knew I would miss Joan. We asked Sister Catherine for permission to spend the day together in York and she said yes. We walked around the town and had lunch and got our photo taken at the photo booth. I knew I was going to miss my friends and especially Joan, and we promised to write to each other and visit each other's home towns for the weekend.

I was glad and sad at the same time to be leaving the school with some good memories. I left school with seven CSEs. My grades were: English – B, Biology – B, Maths – C, Art – B, Cooking – B, History – C, and Typing – C. I did very well and I felt that doing work experience really helped too. I knew exactly what I wanted to do.

It wasn't long after I left school, at 17 years old, only a couple of months later, that my dear friend Joan wrote me a letter and told me some devastating news. Her mother had died in an explosion in a house. I felt so sorry for her and wanted to be there to comfort her, but we were living so far away from each other and I did not have any money. We continued to write to each other and I promised to visit her.

Growing up in my family was wonderful. I have so many

fond and good memories of schooling and holidays. We all were such a close family. My brothers always looked after me and protected me. My parents did their utmost to get me well educated. They didn't have plenty of money, but I always felt that we were all well off. Our home was quite big and always clean. That was because my mother decorated the house herself and kept it clean. She always did a lot of dressmaking for me and my sister and she knitted jumpers for my brothers. We were always smart.

Leaving school, moving onto the next chapter of my life and growing up and facing this huge hearing world was daunting. Basically I was alone, and trying to figure out what I was going to do about work, money, love and children. It was now I realised that it was up to me to make the best of this, and this changed me forever. I had many obstacles to overcome and barriers I would have to break down.

I was an educated young woman who really wanted to work – so where was the help I needed to find this work? This is something I have battled with all my life. I was starting to lose faith in the world. I stopped wearing hearing aids because I hated them. I put them in a drawer in 1978 and have never worn them since.

We moved to another house, this time very newly built. We did not like it very much and I think my parents realised that they had made a mistake. We only lived there for a year and then we moved again to a bigger, older house, in a much nicer area.

All I wanted to do was to work in an office. I did not think about having to use the telephone. I assumed that not being able to use a telephone would have been an issue. Would I have to go to meetings, and how would I cope if I was supposed to take notes? These were things I would not be able to do. I hadn't thought about it really. I did want to work in an office, typing on a typewriter, and I thought it couldn't be that difficult as I had learned to type at school and had some work experience.

Then I discovered the Deaf Club, which used to be a nursery. It was a club for deaf people where we could meet and socialise. It was only one floor and a few toilets. I realised that most of the people I saw there were from Beverley School. I did feel a bit out of place, but I made some friends, and that's where I met Michael, who was also deaf. I didn't like him very much at first, but later he became my boyfriend.

I also made friends with a deaf lady called Enid Thompson. Enid said she could offer me some help in getting me a job using sewing machines in a factory. I wasn't keen about working in a factory but I thought it would be nice to earn some money. My parents were not very keen on me taking on that job, but they did say that if it made me happy then to try it.

After twelve weeks, I hated it! The quicker you worked the more money you earned. It was basically bras and underwear I was working on. I had to attach the hooks onto the backs of the bras – all day, against the clock. You had to write down how many you had done on a ticket to prove how many you had made for the day, so I would try my hardest to work faster.

Sometimes Enid would give me a lift home. Other times, she would invite me to her parents' house, which was only five minutes away from the factory. When I met her parents for the first time, they made me very welcome and took me into the living room. I was so surprised to see her brother and sisters, who were also deaf, on the floor having their tea! It was chips, baked beans and fish fingers and they had their plates on their knees, AND they were watching the television. I never ever did that at home! It was very strange to see that. I realised that working in the factory was not what I wanted to do. I still dreamed of going to work in an office.

I decided to go to the careers office, where I was very surprised to see the lady using sign language. She was excellent. I soon learned that her fiancé was a qualified British Sign Language interpreter and his parents and sister were all deaf. She had had to learn how to communicate with them all. She told me that she sometimes went to the deaf club and she told me her fiancé's sister's name, which I recognised from Beverley School. I asked her for help with getting me an office job, even though I was still working at the factory!

It's not surprising that she was excellent in giving me advice about how to go about getting an office job. She said that I should go to college and recommended Finchale Training College in Durham. She explained that it was a six-month course and I would be able to improve my typing skills, which would help me to get a job in an office. I had just started having a relationship and didn't want to be away from my boyfriend, but I decided to go, and thought six months would soon pass quickly and I would come home every weekend.

I was still working at the factory for about another three weeks, and then I saw my parents in the manager's office.

'What's wrong?' I asked.

'Nothing' said my mother, 'you have got a place at Durham College, starting Monday.'

The manager said it was fine to go and I worked my last shift on the Friday. I was not sorry to be leaving that factory, but I was sorry to say goodbye to Enid. I thanked her very much for her help.

I had to get the bus from the bus station and I arrived at Durham bus station on a Sunday evening, the day before starting my training at Finchale Training College. I was expecting someone from the college to pick me up, but after waiting for half an hour I was starting to get worried as it was getting dark and I couldn't use a phone to call the college. What was I going to do?

I remember I kept on walking and thinking I might have to knock on someone's door and ask for help. I was only seventeen and a half and a bit scared. I remember walking up a path which was very steep, and I had to carry my case up it. I knocked on a door and a young girl opened it. I gave her a piece of paper which had the college's name, phone number and address. She read the note and kindly let me into the house (I remember thinking my parents always warned me not to speak to strangers, never mind going in someone's house!)

There were three other young girls in the house. She introduced them to me and said that they were all studying at Durham University and that this house was student accommodation. She then said she was from London and her next-door neighbours were deaf and that she knew a bit of sign language. What a small world, I thought! Immediately, I felt a bit safer. She kindly called the college and let me wait at their house until someone came for me. It's such a shame that I cannot remember their names.

I found college difficult (it was supposed to be for some people with disabilities) but it wasn't really for deaf people, and we didn't have any interpreter for British Sign Language at the college (at the time there was no equity act for interpreters) and I was not the only deaf person there. However, I did well and made some friends. I did socialise a lot by going to the nearby pubs, although I didn't drink.

After I had been at college for a few weeks I had made some friends, both deaf and hearing. One early evening while I was in my bedroom, I was reading a magazine when all of sudden I looked up to see a girl waving at me from the window trying to get my attention. My room was on about the third floor! I jumped up and shouted, 'What are you doing?'

'Open the door!' she said. I remember her name was Sylvia and she had managed to climb down from the window using the pipe and run around and up the stairs to my room, where she had waited for me to let her into the bedroom. I did find a piece of paper on the floor near the door which she had written on, but my bed was nowhere near the door and I didn't see it because the room was L-shaped. I was amazed!

She said that she had been knocking on the door and kept waiting for me to answer, and then she had realised that I couldn't hear, so she'd had to think of another way to get my attention. 'Crazy woman you are!' I said.

She wanted to ask if I would like to come out for a last drink with them, as they were all going home the next day and had finished their last course. It was very dangerous, yet she had climbed that far just to ask me if I wanted to go for a drink!

Sylvia was a right tomboy at the time, but she was a fabulous friend and we got on well. I did make some other deaf friends during my six months at college. I went home every weekend to see Michael and then return to college but I was very glad to go home after six months' training. I had learned really well how to type and could type at a speed of 65 words per minute. I passed my course.

After I finished college, I went back to the careers office over a four-week period. I saw the same lady who had used sign language when I went originally and she found me employment at the town hall, working on a computer. She made sure that I could work in an office without having to use the telephone and spoke to the employer over a long period of time. She knew exactly what to say to the employer and helped me with the filling in of application forms and speaking to the person in charge of the interview. When I went to the town hall for the interview, I did not have an interpreter and I asked the man and woman who were interviewing me to speak to me slowly and to face me. I felt it went really well and when the interview was about to finish the lady said that 100 people were after this job, but they would send me a letter if they thought I was suitable. Then she took me to the room where all the people were working in the office. I looked around and thought 'no way will I be able to do this job'. It was not typewriters at all but computers instead! What had I learned at college? Typing! But despite my doubts, I did hope to get the job.

One week later and I received a letter… I got the job! My first ever interview! And it was at Middlesbrough Town Hall!

You have no idea how extremely lucky I was to be able to have someone like this lady at the careers office. She treated me like any other person and because she had had some experience with a deaf person, it made the process a lot easier. But we deaf people cannot live on luck.

On my first day at work I was very nervous and wondered how I was going to learn how to use a computer, but if I wanted to do the job, then I would have to. How was I going to do that? The lady next to me showed me how to use the computer, but she had never met a deaf person before. I believe the supervisors must have told her what to do and she showed me how to use the keyboard. I would literally copy numbers and words from a piece of paper onto the computer. It was difficult at first, but I soon got in the swing of things and I started enjoying my new job at last. I was now working in an office!

One of the supervisors showed me a photograph of a deaf lady who used to work at the same office as me and I recognised her. That was probably why they did not see me as any different.

My relationship with Michael had now been going on for about two and a half years. Michael was living with his Uncle Russ at that time, after Uncle Russ's divorce, and I would sometimes go up there and stay at his uncle's house for a few hours, just the two of us. The house was quite nice and was very much like a cottage with an oak ceiling and a huge fire. I would go up sometimes in the evening. I remember one time going up to the house after a long wait for the bus when it was snowing and icy. Uncle Russ would welcome me into the house and take me into the living room, asking if I was all right, helping me to take off my boots and rubbing my feet by the fire to keep them warm. I was extremely uncomfortable at his approaches while Michael looked on and was not too happy about it!

Uncle Russ made me a hot milky drink and kept asking if I was warm enough and if there was anything else he could do for me. I would also be invited to stay for dinner there, and sometimes we got on reasonably well.

One evening when his Uncle Russ was out and we had the house to ourselves, Michael took me upstairs to his uncle's bedroom. He said he wanted to show me something. He said he was suspicious that his uncle was bringing women back to the house, and I thought, well it is his house!

Michael then threw back the bed sheets and I was shocked to see condoms on the bed. I had never seen condoms before and didn't know what to say. Why hadn't they been removed, and why was he doing this at his age?

Michael's auntie too would insist I go to her house for Christmas dinners.

Michael was born deaf because his mother had contracted German measles while she was pregnant with him. She had died when was he was about six years old and his father had never been in his life at all. My parents did not really like Michael very much. They never really had a proper conversation with him, as they could not use British Sign Language, but they felt sorry for him and wanted to welcome him to our family, and we wanted to get married. To help arrange this, Uncle Russ came to my parents' house one evening and said Michael's mother had left him £700, which he suggested should be spent on a deposit for a house and solicitors' fees. We all agreed, but then Uncle Russ put his hand over his mouth and said a few words to my parents while Michael and I looked on, obviously not knowing what he was saying. I still don't know what he said, but I do remember my parents looking astonished and disgusted. My father then said, 'I'm sorry, but please do not put your hands over your mouth when you speak to us'. Uncle Russ did not know what the fuss was about and did not like being told that.

Was I deeply in love with Michael? I don't think I was. I felt sorry for him because he did not have a mother or father and his uncle and aunt had brought him up. I got on fairly well with him and his uncle at first, and he did say I was good for Michael.

CHAPTER THREE

Married Life

We got married at The Holy Name of Mary Catholic Church in Middlesbrough in 1978, and it was a low-key affair. My wedding dress was made by my mother and she also provided the flowers and the wedding cake. Michael's side of the family attended the church with his aunts and uncles. On my way to the church with my father, I remember him saying to me 'I hope he will look after you'. I really wanted to tell him that I had changed my mind because I just felt that I wasn't ready, but I didn't. There had been a lot of effort and work put into the wedding day, so I didn't feel that I could now say I had changed my mind!

We bought our own house with the deposit money that Michael's mother had saved for him. Uncle Russ made sure that Michael used the money wisely. The house was very old; an old lady had moved out of it to live in a nursing home. When we bought it a lot of work needed to be done to it, as all the windows had wooden frames and you had to use ropes between the windows to open them. The two living rooms had different antique fireplaces and one had built-in cupboards, and in the kitchen, which was very basic, there was just a sink and two cupboards. Upstairs in the bathroom there was a Victorian bath, which was not very clean, and the toilet seat was black! There was a square sink and red and cream lino on the floor, and in the back bedroom the wallpaper was green, and so were the dirty curtains. On the stairs there was a long narrow carpet held down at the edges by fluted brass stair-rods. In the front bedroom there was an antique fireplace and a worn brown carpet, and the hall was decorated with ugly flowered wallpaper.

My father painted all the outside windows of the house and I scraped the wallpaper off. Michael wallpapered the hall, though he made a mess of it, and my mother papered the living room. To make the living room bigger my brother David knocked down the wall himself and Stephen's friend, who was a joiner, came round to put in a lintel to secure the wall. We paid for someone to fit the bathroom with a new bath, toilet and sink. The very old Victorian bath had black rings all around it and no matter how hard I tried to get rid of it I could not.

We put the bath out in the alley and someone knocked on the door to ask if they could have the taps! We did not understand what the man was trying to say at first. I said 'I don't understand you, please say again slowly'.' Sorry', said the man, and when he repeated it we understood. We said he could have the taps. We did wonder why he wanted them, because we thought they were ugly.

About a week later the bath was still in the alley, without the taps, and then two men rang the bell and asked if they could take the bath! I understood straight away because he was pointing to the alley. We were more than happy to get rid of it, so the men took it.

While we were busy in the house we did not really get to know any of the neighbours, but then one day an elderly woman from the house on our right opened our front door (I think she must have knocked and waited for a bit before deciding to open it) and brought us a tray of sandwiches and a pot of tea and cups! She even lent us a knife and fork and spoons!

As she walked into the living room she said 'Here is something small for both of you and my name is… oh dear, I can't remember!' She handed us the tray and said if we needed anything please don't hesitate. She was a good neighbour over the years that followed.

I liked the area, as it was close to the church and the park and only a short walk to my grandmother's and the supermarket. Soon our house was coming along nicely and it was cleaner with my family all running around helping with the improvements. My father even took out the antique fireplace in the front bedroom and bricked up the wall and plastered it. My family rallied around helping with the house, which really helped us to save our money in a big way. But where was Michael's family when we needed their help with the house?

My parents also helped to sort out the solicitor's fees and made several phone calls helping with the paperwork. Michael had cousins, uncles and aunties but we never saw them. For our wedding present, my parents paid for the rewiring of the whole house and my grandmother give me £400 which we used for a new carpet in the living room. That helped to make our house comfortable and safe.

Before we got married, Michael lived there on his own for a few weeks. After the wedding, I moved in with him and we made it a nice home. I continued working at the town hall and still enjoyed it.

Then Uncle Russ came to see Michael to inform him that he had found him a job as a welder at Scunthorpe. I was not very happy about this as there was work for welders twenty minutes away from our house. Uncle Russ claimed it was a favour from a friend he knew. The new job meant Michael would come home at the weekend and return to work each Sunday night by train, while I stayed home and went to work. This went on for a few months until I managed to find him a job at Remploy doing welding work. There were many other people there with different disabilities and deaf people worked there too. The money was not the same as he could earn at Scunthorpe, but we were together and that was the main thing.

We made more improvements on our house, getting rid of the antique fireplaces in the living rooms and replacing them with two wooden gas fires that fixed onto the walls. Michael knew someone who did joinery and he mentioned that we could do with new windows. We did have some money in the bank and I agreed to have new windows for the whole house and a new kitchen.

We both worked hard and saved up the money for these things. I earned more money than he did, but that didn't matter. However, after a few months, I did notice that he liked to drink. I don't drink, but I do enjoy going out to socialise. I saved up enough to get him a car and paid for his driving lessons, but I then got worried, as he would drink and drive.

After we had been married for about five years, I became pregnant. I did think then that Michael would change his ways, grow up a little and look after me. I also thought that he would have the sense not to drink and drive any more. I hated him smoking in the house as I cannot stand the smell of cigarettes.

When I was seven months pregnant, like any first-time mother, I was excited and was saving up for things. I prepared the baby's room and bought clothes, a pram and a cot etc. I even got my small case ready to take to the hospital (toothpaste, flannel, soap, nightdress etc). Just one thing was missing that hearing people would never have to think about – I thought I'd better go and see the social worker for the deaf, to ask if there was any sort of special lamp for deaf people that would flash when the baby was crying. I had learned that these lamps existed and wanted to ask for one.

When I met her for the first time I thought the social worker's sign language was very poor. She seemed to be making it up as she went along. I remember thinking that the lady at the careers office was 20 times better. Did she attend British Sign Language classes, or any deaf awareness training courses? Or have an understanding of deaf culture? I suspected that she had never done these courses.

I wanted a flashing lamp with microphone near the cot, so that if the baby cried in the middle of the night needing to be fed, it would wake me up. The social worker said I couldn't have one and asked how far I was. I said seven months, and she said 'come back when the time gets closer' and looked at me as if I was being silly. I thought 'Who does she think she is? When am I supposed to come back? Why should I have to do that? Was she right to refuse?'

I told her Michael was also deaf. I did not like her attitude and refused to leave the room. I demanded that the flashing light lamp was sorted there and then. She was taken aback and looked at me in surprise. She was reluctant, but then she agreed to fill in the form and I was told to return in two weeks' time to pick it up. When I went back to pick it up, the social worker didn't say anything other than to ask me to sign the paperwork.

I was worried about going to hospital, because how would the nurses and doctors communicate with me? I was also worried about the first time giving birth. I did not need anything else to add my anxiety.

On the 28th September 1983, early afternoon, I began to feel uncomfortable. I was full term at this point and I had really bad back pains. By the time Michael came home from work, I couldn't eat my tea, but he ate his and said he was going out with his friends, even though I told him I was not feeling too well. I asked him not to go out, as I was scared of being home alone when it was my first time being pregnant and so close to going into labour. I was huge!

He told me I would be fine. I asked him not to go again and not to have too many drinks, and he just shrugged his shoulders.

I started to have contractions more frequently and I was extremely uncomfortable, and to add more worries, I knew that I would have to face Michael's drunkenness when he returned home. I had not slept and when he returned and went to sleep I didn't try too hard to wake him up as I knew he would lose his temper.

As the night progressed, I kept looking at Michael on our bed, hoping he would wake. When he eventually did wake up he could not keep his balance. I needed to him to go to my brother Stephen's house, which was only few streets away, so he could call an ambulance for us and call my parents. I was in a lot of pain and unhappy with Michael for his behaviour because he had gone out that evening and left me alone all night while he boozed and then arrived home heavily drunk while I was having contractions.

I was in hospital overnight and Michael slept on the chair while I kept walking around the room. He woke up and said 'I'm going home, I will return later', which he did, but I was still in labour. He then said he was leaving again! I had been in labour for 27 hours when he returned, drunk again. When I was in the room ready to give birth, he went to sleep.

I never got any flowers or a card from Michael, either when I was in hospital or when I got home. My mother asked my brother Stephen to get me some flowers which I could put up on top of my drawers at the hospital, and when Michael saw them he did not know what to say.

Our son, Philip, was born on 1st October 1983. The hospital was very small with only two wards, one for mothers who smoked on the left side wing and the other, on the right, for those who did not smoke. It was ideal for deaf mothers, as there were plenty of nurses, so they had more time for you.

I was worried about the night time, when I might be asleep if Philip needed to be fed, so I asked one of the nurses to wake me up when he cried. She said she would, but she didn't. It was the lady next to me who woke me up to tell me my baby was crying, and I got very upset as I could see that he had been crying for some time. I had to go to another room to breastfeed Philip and I got angry and upset with the nurse for forgetting to wake me up. She apologised.

While I was breast-feeding Philip there was a baby asleep alone wrapped in a blue blanket, and I asked the nurse where his mother was. She told me his mother already had three children and did not want to take him home, and I thought how sad. I was extremely lucky, for at least there was one nurse who could use British Sign Language. She told me that her grandparents were deaf and she had learned it from them when she was growing up.

After a few days I was discharged. I arrived home to see a pile of clothes on the table. Michael said that he had left them for me to iron! I could not believe it. I could barely walk and was still feeling weak. We did not have any money as he had spent it all on booze.

I was not happy at home and my feelings for Michael had changed. I felt I wanted to keep away from him, but at the same time, I did not really understand why I felt like that.

I started to use the flashing light for the first time (it was a very sensitive lamp - if you even coughed slightly it would flash very quickly). I loved being a mother looking after this little person who was so content. I was breast-feeding and got well into a routine. I knew I would be lost without the lamp, but after I had used it without any problems for a month it suddenly stopped working. I did not sleep that night. I panicked and went to the social worker who had given me the lamp. I did not want to see her, but she was the only person who was available who could help me. I was at her office first thing at 9 am, with Philip in his pram. I walked all the way to the office to ask for a replacement lamp.

I could see she was unmoved, and she told me to fill the forms in and come back next week. 'Next week?' I said, 'No I want a replacement now!' Didn't the social worker wonder how on earth I was going to be able to wake up during the night? Of course not, even though she had three children herself. Philip was only four weeks old.

Michael told me that feeding the baby was my job and that he had to get up for work. I thought perhaps he would leave his hearing aid on and listen for me, but he did not want to be disturbed. If I dared to ask him to listen for Philip's cry, I knew he would lose his temper.

I wondered what I was going to do. How on earth was I going to wake up to feed him during the night? The only way I could think of doing it was to move the cot closer to my bed and sleep with my arm in between the rails with my hand on my son's chest all night, every night for a week. It was November and we didn't have central heating. My hands were freezing!

I kept waking up and checking the clock for his next feed (I was still breast-feeding). I didn't sleep a wink for a week and was deprived of any sleep. I could not sleep during the day either. On the day when the new lamp was ready to be collected, I was at the door of the social worker's office at 8.45 am. I couldn't wait to get the flashing lamp and get away from that social worker. Did she ask how I had managed for a week? Certainly not!

It was heaven when I got the flashing lamp and I could sleep and keep my hand warm! I was very careful with the lamp after that and did not have any more trouble with it, thankfully.

A few months later I realised I needed an alarm clock, but

again not the standard type. I went see the same social worker as before – I didn't want to, but I had no choice. I explained that I wanted to get up earlier so that I would be able to get ready before my son got up, but she refused to let me have one as I was not in full-time employment. Typical!

Michael did have a vibration alarm clock under his pillow for him to get up early for work but I didn't want to rely on him waking me. Also I preferred an alarm clock that had a flashing light built into it. This type is specially made for deaf people. It is an electric alarm clock with a light that flashes on and off instead of a noise. My mother and I went to many shops around the town looking for this type of alarm clock and we eventually found one. It was old and dated, but it was better than nothing. As expected it didn't last very long, and I was unable to replace the bulb, although I searched for one, so I just had to do without.

As part of the baby's growth development I would regularly see the same health visitor who had come to my home when he had been a few days old to check on his weight and growth. I would take him to the surgery to see her to check on his development, vision, growth and speech. I expected her to be qualified and to have undertaken further training and education in child health and given immunizations at the same time. When Philip was nine months old I went to see her, and it was always the same one; I never saw any other health visitors. I could not understand why on that particular morning she invited me to sit on a chair which was placed very close to the door and facing it, with colourful charts on it. I did not like it and felt a bit uncomfortable. No explanation was given beforehand, but I did sit on it and she put Philip on my lap and said 'do not move'. I sat looking and facing the door, and Philip was so excited at looking at the colours.

I waited for a couple of minutes, wondering what on earth what was going on. Then she turned me around to face her. She was holding a bunch of car keys.

'I am very sorry, but Philip is deaf' she said. That word will haunt me forever. I refused to believe she was right. It just seemed like such a lazy diagnosis, shaking a bunch of keys once. Just because Philip did not react she was very quick to suggest that he was deaf, and that was that.

I went home and burst into tears, and I cried and cried. Then I put Philip into his pram and walked for about 20 minutes to my mother's, looking at Philip and thinking 'My beautiful baby is deaf'. So many thoughts raced through my mind, and the worst thought of all was that he would have to go to Beverley school.

I arrived at my mother's house very upset and told her what had happened.

'What are you talking about?' she said. 'There is nothing wrong with Philip's hearing, he is coming along really well with his development!'

We made an appointment the following day to see the same health visitor together; she greeted us with smiles, not realizing how angry we were about the bombshell she had dropped so unsympathetically. My mother immediately said, 'There is nothing wrong with Philip's hearing' and told her how angry she was. She explained that Philip's speech was coming on normally and that he could hear fine, as she had been taping him talking and having conversations through a microphone and tape recorder! The health visitor just said 'Is he?' 'Yes' said my mother.

I felt so reassured when my mother stuck up for me. It was like a massive weight being lifted from my shoulders! The health visitor seemed embarrassed and very apologetic.

I still felt unhappy with my marriage at this point as Michael seemed to want to enjoy the single lifestyle, and was out with his friends and boozing all the time. We didn't have much money as I was a housewife looking after our son and had decided not to return to work. We needed to be careful and manage with money, but he was only interested in wasting it on drink and cigarettes. He would regularly come home at all hours of the night, and I got scared of him as he would be very aggressive when he was drunk.

One night I could not sleep knowing he would come home drunk and unable to balance. I was half asleep when the hall light came on and I pretended to be asleep but I could see what he was doing. He opened my wardrobe and instead of using the toilet he urinated all over my clothes! I went back to sleep very afraid and kept still. I had to wait till the morning to confront him. I knew there would be no point arguing, as I had learned that you cannot reason with a drunk person.

The next morning I was angry and pointed at the clothes, which stank of urine. He just shrugged and told me 'wash them, it will be fine'. He didn't care or apologize. He behaved as though it was nothing. I had to take nearly all the clothes out and wash, hang and iron them all, then put them away in the wardrobe, which I also had to clean.

There were other times when he would climb into bed after his night out drinking and urinate in there. I would have to go downstairs and sleep on the sofa, which was extremely uncomfortable, and wait till morning. I would have to have another argument, this time about the bed, and he would say 'clean it and leave the window open, it will dry out itself'.

I wasn't sleeping very well and one night, I woke up at three o' clock in the morning. Michael was not in bed. I got worried as he did drink and drive. I got out of bed to see if he was downstairs and found him in the bathroom sitting on the toilet, asleep, with his trousers down. I couldn't move him and I thought, 'What am I going to do?'

I thought I'd better leave him there and go back to bed, though I was very unsettled about it. He must have woken up and come into bed some time in the night because he was there when I woke up the next morning.

Sometimes I would lie awake and wait for him to come home, as he would be drinking and driving. I knew when he arrived because I could see car lights outside our house and then the hall light would come on. I would then pretend to be asleep. I hated it when he used to come into bed because I had to put up with this very strong, unpleasant smell and he would be stinking of beer.

One time I woke up at seven o'clock on my own. I quickly went downstairs to the living room and found him fast asleep on the armchair. I woke him up and he was angry with me and went upstairs to bed. I noticed that the armchair was covered in his urine and there was an ash tray full of cigarettes. At no point did I ask him about the armchair. I just cleaned it.

I then suggested that he should sell the car as we were struggling with money. He did not want to at first, but then he agreed to get rid of it. In a way, it was better, because no matter how many times I told him that he should not be drinking and driving, he carried on. He did not care. One time I hid his car keys, and he was furious. It got to the point when I did not care if he came home at all, because I had had enough. There were two occasions when he came home with his face covered in bruises because he had been beaten up by some men when he was walking home, but at that point, I honestly couldn't care less.

At one stage Philip would climb out of his cot and come to our bedroom a few times during the night, and Michael would be furious and throw him back into his cot. I was terrified, as Philip got very upset and so did I. One time I had had enough and I went next door to ask them to call the police, but they said they didn't have a telephone, so I went back to the house very upset. Michael was laughing and teasing me.

Only two days after that, my mother came to my house one afternoon and said 'what is going on with that phone next door? It never stops ringing. They must be out'. That's when I knew they had lied and didn't care that I had a disability that prevented me from using the phone myself, or that I had a baby.

During that summer, Philip developed eczema on his legs and he was wearing shorts. I asked Michael to take him to the corner shop for some milk, but he refused and asked me to put trousers on him to cover up his legs before taking him to the shop as he was embarrassed! How could he do that to his own flesh and blood?

I went to the doctor's as I had missed my period. I very much hoped that I wasn't pregnant again, but the doctor confirmed that I was. I was so shocked. I asked for another test but he said no.

There followed a difficult nine months, as this wasn't planned. Michael promised to cut down on his drinking and try to give up smoking. He did manage it, but only for about two weeks, then he went back to the same routine all over again. He promised he would stay at home and if I went into labour he would walk around to my brother Stephen's house and get him to call an ambulance.

This time I didn't want Michael to be with me during the birth. I was in labour eleven hours and for most of the time I was on my own. My mother looked after Philip, as I was not comfortable leaving him with Michael.

Our second son, Jamie, was born on February 21st. The midwife was a lovely nurse and she told all the other mothers at this hospital that I was deaf and to treat me like a normal person. She made sure that the nurse remembered to wake me up during the night if Jamie needed to be fed. She could use British Sign Language, and she was a lovely nurse who had been married herself for seven years and badly wanted a family. Sadly she died a year later from cancer. I wanted to visit her, but she refused any visitors.

Michael once again promised to be more sensible with his drinking and would go outside if he needed to smoke, as I did not want him smoking in the house with Philip and Jamie there. He agreed to that, but he did not control his drinking. On the mornings before he went to work he would try to kiss me, but I would turn away as I felt sick. He would just look at me and laugh.

For some reason when I was in bed one morning and Michael was getting ready for work, I looked at him and thought, 'My God, isn't he ugly!' I would feel sick if he came near me or tried to kiss me. I could not really understand why I was feeling like that. I just wanted to be kept away from him.

CHAPTER FOUR

Single mother

When Jamie was twelve weeks old I started thinking about divorce. I felt it would be better for Philip and Jamie and I also thought this was a way to protect them. I decided I did want a divorce, and I confronted Michael about it. He looked at me and laughed and said 'You wouldn't go ahead and do that, would you?'

It didn't go well at all when he told his Uncle Russ of the situation, because Russ then turned up at our house shortly after. We were surprised, as we had never seen him since our wedding. He never came to see how Michael and I were getting on and if we needed any help. This was the first time I had seen him, and I confronted him and refused to let him in the house. I said 'Stay where you are on the doorstep'. I was really angry with him. He came right up to my face, pointing his finger at me, and said 'I am going to make absolutely sure that you, Philip and baby Jamie are going to be thrown out of the house. I have got a solicitor and he is a friend of mine and we are going to fight tooth and nail to have you out of the house'. He then reminded me that the money we had used as a deposit for the house was from Michael's mother and that she had saved up the money for him. He was furious with me. His attitude toward me was unbelievable. He actually believed that I did not deserve to stay in the house and it was right that Michael would have his money if I were to move out.

Didn't Uncle Russ once say to me 'you are good for him?' Now he was all against me. What was I supposed to have done to Michael? All this was going on after I had just put Philip and Jamie to bed upstairs. I was extremely upset and frightened that I would have to be removed from the house, and worried what would happen to three of us. I didn't sleep for a very long time while all this was going around in my head.

I did not have a solicitor. I found one in Yellow Pages, but my mother got in touch with the Citizens' Advice Bureau to ask them for help, and they said they would send us a list of solicitors and we could choose one. I was not very happy with the solicitor we saw. My mother called him and explained that I was deaf and that she would be coming along for support. While we were there, he would look at his watch every five minutes, which was making us uncomfortable.

Each time I had to see him I would have to tell my mother what had been going on between me and Michael and she would write everything down and come with me to the solicitor's office while my father looked after Philip and Jamie. While we were at the solicitor's office, he would leave the door open with his secretary next door so she could hear what my mother was saying. I did not think it was right, and felt we had no privacy. When we walked out of the office when we had finished our discussion I noticed that the secretary's surname on her desk was Bland – I thought this was strange as my maiden name was Bland.

Michael and Uncle Russ were using a firm of solicitors opposite my solicitor's office. Michael went along with everything his uncle said. He didn't put up a fight and say that the children would be better off in the house.

A few weeks later it was time to go to court. On the day of the case, we had to travel to a court in Hartlepool, which my father drove us to. Michael and his uncle were there and Russ said to me evilly, 'you will not be getting the house'. He made sure I understood that. He said 'I am going to wait here on this chair till you come out of that room'.

There was only one interpreter for us, arranged by Russ for me and Michael. I had a photograph of a bruise on my back, which Michael had caused, and gave it to the solicitor. Michael admitted that he had done it.

I had to leave Philip and Jamie with my parents' next-door neighbours while my parents drove me to the court. Michael was still adamant that I should be put into a council house and have our house sold and divide the money between us. He wasn't interested in fighting for the children. The Judge asked Michael, 'You want her to leave her home and live in a council house with your children?' 'Yes' said Michael, but the Judge ordered that I was entitled to the house and contents till I remarried, co-habited or sold it. He decided that because I had the children and their welfare came first, I should live there. He ordered Michael to pay the mortgage, which was £10 a month for seven years (that was when the house would be paid for).

The Judge then decided that Michael would have Philip and Jamie on Saturdays from one o'clock till five as custody on those days only, and if he wanted to see them more (to have them the whole weekend) then he would have to ask me. The court decided to put an injunction on him, and he was given 28 days to find somewhere else to live.

I knew that his aunts and uncles had houses with plenty of rooms within their homes, but not one of them offered Michael a room. I believe they did this on purpose, hoping that I would not be able to cope with him in the house and agree to move out myself. This meant I would have to co-habit with Michael for 28 days before he had to find somewhere else to live.

What was I going to do? I did think I could not bear it with a baby and a two-year-old child, but I did not have a choice. I decided that I had to make sure to use the kitchen when he went to work or when he went out. To use the bathroom I would keep out of his way until it was free, so I could look after Philip and the baby if I needed to, or use the bath. Every morning I would look out of my upstairs bedroom window and wait for him to go to work. Jamie's cot was in there, and a small bed made for Philip because we shared my bedroom, while Michael used the back bedroom. Then I would come downstairs and use the house the way I liked it until he was due back from work. I would get on with looking after the children, feeding them, dressing them, and then leave the house go to my mother's for our tea before Michael came home. We would not see each other, and when we all returned from my mother's I would check that Michael was not in the house, then put the pram in the hall and get the boys ready for bed. Then we all stayed in my bedroom with a bolt across the door to keep Michael out.

This did not stop Michael going out boozing with his friends or worrying about looking for somewhere to live. He couldn't care less and he would return drunk night after night. I was worried for my life, for Philip and Jamie. I put up a calendar in the kitchen so that we could both see he had so many days remaining before he had to go, and I put big red crosses on the days gone by every day to count the days down. Philip, Jamie and I continued to share my bedroom, doing the same thing for 28 days. I would look out of the bedroom window and wait for him to leave the house so we could go downstairs and do the housework or play. It was important to do this as I didn't want the children to feel restricted in the house.

When Michael came home from work I would go to my mother's for a couple of hours, where I would have tea, wash and bath the children. When I eventually came home I would go to our bedroom, put Philip and Jamie to sleep and bolt the door, as Michael slept in the back bedroom. We did that for 28 days, until the day came when he was forced to leave the house. Did Michael put his children first? He hardly saw them for 28 days!

Michael and his Uncle Russ were hoping I would give up the house so that he could have the money. The children were not his priority, and I don't call him a father. I detested Michael seeing them, but I had no choice. I was so thankful that the Judge had decided that I could live in the house so I could raise Philip and Jamie without being scared and trying to have a normal life without having to rely on my parents all the time.

I could not wait to see Russ' face when I walked out of court. I said to him 'I am not going anywhere and I am staying at that house', and it felt so good saying that to him! He certainly wasn't pleased – he never said a word! He immediately went over to his solicitor. I was pleased that I could stay at the house and no more looking out of the window all the time. The best thing was that Philip and Jamie could go back to their bedroom.

The day he had to leave the house, I said 'I'll help you pack your clothes and carry your suitcases out of the house for you'. I waved the calendar at his face, because finally the day had come! Because I had the house, I asked if he wanted the table, chairs and television. He said he did and took them with him to a house that his Uncle Russ found for him, but I never thought he would actually take them.

For the first time in a month I was able to relax and move freely around the house. It didn't dawn on me that I was on my own with a five-month old baby and a little boy, no dining table or chairs, no television, no telephone, no car and very little money after the bills, but I still had my twin tub washing machine, which I really needed, especially washing the nappies every day!

We had to eat our breakfast, dinner and tea on the sofa. We would just have to manage without the television for a while. As soon as Philip and Jamie were in bed I would go to bed too.

The first few nights after Michael moved out, he would call around in the evening and ask me to reconsider. He promised he would change his behaviour and said he was sorry for all the aggravation he had put us all through over the past couple of months, but I wasn't interested. I felt that I was now safe and certainly didn't want to go through all that again. I said 'No, please do not call around here again'. He did this four nights in a row, and I eventually say 'if you keep harassing me again I am going to get the police' (not really knowing how I would manage to get them to come). He never came around again after I said that.

Over the next few months I managed to save up for a second-hand table and chairs from a charity shop. I carefully worked out that I could afford to pay for a television on a weekly payment scheme from the little money I had. I was glad to be able to stay at the house as I felt it was a home for the three of us. This was just the type of stability I've wanted all along.

It was arranged by the court that Michael would have visiting rights on Saturday afternoons from 1pm-5pm. I was dreading every Saturday, when he would come for Philip and Jamie. I put Jamie in his pushchair and got Philip ready and had them at the front door. Michael never stepped inside the house. I decided it would be best to let the boys go outside the door as soon as Michael arrived. Then when they returned home I would open the door and let them in without any words between me and Michael. I would be really glad to see them and give the boys a hug and kiss, because I had been without them for the afternoon. I never asked them any questions about their afternoon with their father or anything.

There were times when I used to get them ready and he would not turn up! We used to play a game while we were waiting for him - 'Do this' putting my arms across or 'Do that!' if one of them got it wrong it would be 'you're out of the game!' It was a 'Simon Says' type of game, but the aim was to copy everything I did when saying 'do this' but when I said 'do that' and you did it, you would be out. I was trying to keep their minds occupied as to not get them upset. But if he did not turn up, I would take them out myself.

One time it was Jamie's birthday and Michael turned up without a birthday present. I had to remind him! The following week he arrived with a Ghostbusters van, which Jamie absolutely loved.

Michael would come most weekends, but he never once gave me any money towards the kids' new shoes or new coats for the winter. He would spend his money on drinks or cigarettes. At this point, there was no law to make fathers or mothers pay child support for their children.

He would sometimes bring Philip and Jamie back within two hours and tell me he was bored. But it was different when he had a new girlfriend, because he would turn up and drop them off after the full five hours. He had wanted to show this new girlfriend what a great father he was!

One Saturday when he turned up to pick up the children, he was very angry with me. He said 'Why have you reported me to the CSA?' I didn't know what he was talking about; I hadn't reported him to anyone. I told him this, but he didn't seem to believe me. It turns out that Margaret Thatcher had created the Child Support Agency in 1990, and in 1993 it became law that child support was paid. It cost him £5 a month for each child. Michael never apologised or brought it up again.

Michael's girlfriends would come and go, but he saw one particular one for a while and I knew she wasn't deaf. One day I saw this woman standing on the other side of the street just staring at my house. I thought nothing of it at first, but when I realised she was still just standing looking at the house I began to wonder who she was and what she wanted. For about five or ten minutes she still was standing there. I ran upstairs to get a better view of her and it then became clear that she was pregnant. I went back to the living room and then opened the curtains and waved her off. She just walked away.

I did find that very strange and wondered if Michael was going to be a father again. Then a couple of months later she was standing at the same spot looking at the house again, but this time she had a baby in a pram. I did not want to know. At first I just ignored her, but she did not move, so I opened the net curtains and waved her off again. I have no idea why she did this or what had happened to her, and I never saw her again.

Not very long afterwards Michael brought a new girlfriend a few times, and I was shocked when I had got Philip and Jamie ready to take them to the door to see that this woman had a big bruise on the left side of her face. I did not say anything, but I was not surprised. He asked if Philip and Jamie could go to his wedding, as he was getting married again. I refused to allow this as I was not sure how well Philip and Jamie would be looked after in a room full of strange people, and no one at the wedding would know our sons well.

His new wife was already pregnant with his child. When he picked Philip and Jamie up for his Saturday 'duty', as I called it, he was delighted to announce that he had had a baby daughter! This meant that Philip and Jamie now had both a half-brother and half sister by then. Did I want to know? I wasn't the slightest bit interested!

Michael was now already a father of four. I was very uncomfortable and very unhappy about having Philip and Jamie at his house with his new wife, as I knew the area was a bit rough and he did have a very big dog. I gave him a list of foods that

Jamie could or couldn't have to eat, and warned him that both Philip and Jamie could not go near dogs or cats. However when Jamie returned I noticed he was not very well. I was very concerned and kept myself awake all night checking on Jamie. I was worried, as Jamie was wheezing and his eyes were all puffed up during the night. I kept very calm and took all of us to the hospital, where I was told he had to stay overnight.

The following week when Michael came for them I explained that I had had to take Jamie to hospital because he was allergic to the dog. I had already told him about keeping the dog away and I held him responsible. 'Oh well, he's fine now isn't he?' was his response.

He never knew that I had taken Jamie to hospital for treatment for his asthma and never questioned or took any interest.

Then on his Saturday babysitting he started coming on his own, and told me he was no longer married and was getting divorced again after less than a year of marriage. He did not see his daughter.

When Philip was starting school full time I went to see Michael at his friend's flat. At that time I was struggling with money. When I asked if he was going to pay for Philip's school uniform he said no. After that I never asked him for anything ever again.

Shortly after that he met a woman who was a lot older than him. I thought she was not very pretty and that somehow I recognized her from somewhere, but I couldn't put my finger on it. Michael went to live with her at her house and when Philip and Jamie came back from there Philip said her surname was Bland. That's when I knew – she was that secretary I had seen when I went to the solicitor for my divorce.

I was astonished to realise that this woman must have listened to our conversations and typed letters to be sent to me, all about the bruises and the house, all the things he had done to me, and yet she was willing to have a relationship with him. She would sometimes come with Michael in her car, and sometimes he would come with her daughter. She had a daughter and grandchildren and a son slightly older than my sons and Michael was living with her for nothing, as I later found out. Philip and Jamie would and stay at her house for couple of hours, and it was difficult because her son had everything, but as we did not have the luxury of having the best toys and games, her son James would enjoy rubbing his nose to them (I have recently found out about it and that really hurts me) because he had all the best stuff.

It was not long afterwards that the boys started telling me they did not enjoy seeing their father on Saturdays because they found it boring having to stay in the house watching television. Michael did not take them anywhere. He was giving them one pound pocket money each. Then one Saturday before Michael came for them Philip said 'I don't want to go with my dad today, I want to play with my friends'. By then he was about 10 years old. I said. 'That's fine, if that is what you want to do'. Philip looked at me in a surprise. 'Go and play with your friends' I said. He asked Jamie to tell his father that he was not going to be with him today.

Then I asked Jamie what he wanted to do and he said he wanted to go with Dad. I said that was fine. Jamie continued to see his dad for a little while, and Michael continued giving him a pound pocket money and nothing for Philip. Then Jamie too decided not to see him any more. I would be lying if I said I wasn't delighted. It was their decision and was entirely up to them.

Then Michael's girlfriend Maureen came to the door and said 'I am going to take you to court because Michael has every right to see them. I know what I am talking about, I work for the solicitor'. Did I lose any sleep over it? Certainly not! Did she keep her words? Of course not. What did Michael say? Absolutely nothing.

I did find being a single mother very hard, but I just had to get on with it. We didn't have the luxury of toys and games like Playstation or Gameboy, or a small television or computer of the kind most boys would have in their bedroom. I had to get on with it and bring my sons up the best possible way I could. They are the centre of my world. I would walk through fire for them; I would walk on burning coals barefoot for them.

When Jamie was seven months old his skin developed a very bad eczema. I took him to the doctors and wrote on a bit of paper to explain the problem, and he was given cream to be rubbed gently all over the body from the neck all the way to his feet. and I was told not to use any soap when he had his baths. I used the cream three times a day, and some nights I would wake up to comfort him as he would scratch his skin and bleed (there was a long lead from the flashing lamp in my bedroom to his).

After a while I didn't think the cream was helping him, so I decided to take him back to the doctor's. When he saw me he immediately wrote me a prescription even before I opened my month! I wrote a note telling the doctor I wanted more help about his skin, but he must have thought I was an over-reacting mother. He asked if I would like to see a dietician, and I said yes.

My mother and I went along to see the dietician and my mother explained that I was deaf and told her about Jamie's skin condition. When she saw me she looked at me as if she had never met a deaf person before. I get that all the time!

She examined Jamie's skin and explained to us that the food I was giving him could cause his skin to develop soreness. She gave me a list of food items and their contents, preservatives, additives and E numbers. We were surprised, as we had never known about this and I was making baby food myself to save money. I had to learn and read the labels on every food and change the way I made the food. Slowly and gradually Jamie's skin began to improve, and it was wonderful to see him looking more healthy, with a smooth skin. He was now a happier baby and I did not have to wake up through the night. I had been right to persuade the doctor.

For Jamie's development checks I regularly went to see the same health visitor, and I was apprehensive at having to see the same one when she was checking his growth, his vision and his weight for a few months. Nothing was said about his hearing, but one day when I arrived she said to me, 'I am sorry but there is something wrong with his speech and he is not saying anything much'. At 20 months old? She suggested that he would have to see a speech therapist as his speech was not coming on at all. Again I was very upset. I straight away went to see my mother and she could not believe it. 'What is she talking about?' she said. 'There's nothing with wrong with his speech, it's coming along fine! What it is about this health visitor? Don't worry, when you have the appointment I will go with you.'

When we went to see the speech therapist I took Jamie's favourite book and the security blanket that he always had with him, and we sat with the lady again. Once again she looked at me as if she had never seen a deaf person before. My mother explained that I was deaf and there was nothing wrong with Jamie's speech and that he read books with my mother without any problems. But when she produced his favourite book Jamie was stubborn, and refused to say one word!

It was so funny during that half an hour with the speech therapist that Jamie refused to say a word and clutched his favourite book onto his chest, refusing to let it go! Eventually he did manage to say 'car' and 'pup' (cup), but he was only one and a half years old. Did he have speech problems? No! In fact he soon turned into quite a chatterbox.

We were told there and then that we would not require another appointment. Why was this? Was I being judged just because I was a deaf mother? What does that have to do with anything? Was the health visitor right? Was she being professional? Did she know exactly what she was talking about? Judge for yourself. It was all absolutely unnecessary and it caused me a lot of heartache and anxiety for nothing.

I believed in routine and discipline. I would always make sure the boys had their feeds and sleeps at the same time every day, with baths before bed, and I would read stories to them before they went to sleep. I never smacked my sons as I didn't think it was necessary, and I never used dummies as I didn't see the need. I absolutely loved looking after them and I always made sure they were clean, fed and happy.

One day when Jamie was about two years old he came into my bedroom looking pale and ill. I couldn't understand why, and noticed his breathing was not normal. I panicked, walking around the house and wondering how I could get a doctor. It was two o'clock in the morning and all I could think of was write down the phone number and to knock my next door neighbour's door. I did feel awful for waking her up as she was an old lady (bless her, she has since died). I asked her to call the doctor. She only opened the door a little – not that I blamed her at that hour. I gave her the paper with the doctor's telephone number and she opened the door and asked me for some money!

As I waited I got more worried looking at Jamie wheezing. When the doctor arrived at our house communication was difficult, which didn't help the situation as I got more upset and frustrated. When the paramedics arrived again there was a breakdown in communication as they were asking me a lot of questions. We were all taken to hospital, only to be faced with more questions from the nurse and doctor about what was wrong with Jamie.

Then I was told Jamie had to be kept in overnight. Philip and I went home, and when I returned I had to take Philip to the hospital because I could not leave him on his own at home. It was horrible to have to put Philip in his bedroom without Jamie.

The next day when I went to the hospital my father was there and spoke to the doctor, who told me that Jamie had asthma. I was very upset, but I could see he was improving with medication, and he was allowed home.

I received a letter to attend the outpatient department at the hospital for Jamie's asthma treatment. When we met the doctor, he told my mother that he had never met a deaf person before and said he would like to learn. I was amazed that he wanted to learn, as it's very rare to hear a doctor say that. Some of the nurses had attended classes to learn British Sign Language and he was happy for the nurse to come in the room after Jamie's checks up on his health. He always took his time and was happy for me to ask questions, and he always made sure I understood the medication fully. I have never met another doctor like him. He was a wonderful doctor and wanted to help in every way he could.

Jamie was given quite a lot of medication and a nebulizer, which he had to use three times a day. I was bit nervous about giving Jamie those medications, as I wanted to do it right. I explained that it was difficult for me to get help when Jamie had an asthma attack as I would have to ask my neighbour, then wait for the doctor, then the ambulance, then to be taken to hospital.

Dr Wyatt listened and said he would write a letter so that next time Jamie needed the hospital I would only need to go straight to the hospital with the letter and show it to the receptionist. That would help to make things easier for Jamie and myself. Philip too was developing asthma and I required them both go to the hospital to see Dr Wyatt. I have never forgotten what he did for all of us.

As Philip and Jamie were growing up I was very careful with the little money I had and I always made sure that they was plenty of food on the table, plenty of warmth and clothes so they did look smart and clean at all times. They didn't have fancy brands like Reebok or Nike. As far as toys and computer games were concerned I was not able to afford them as other families did, but I did my best at Christmas time and birthdays.

We went on holiday to Whitby one year and stayed in an apartment the next year. We went to Haven in a caravan; my father drove us there. We have wonderful memories of those times. The holiday was paid for by the church from a charity organization.

When my sister had a car she would take us to Preston Park, Saltburn or Redcar at weekends in the summer. Sometimes we would take a picnic with my nieces. My mother would wallpaper my house for me to keep the house homely and my father did some painting outside to keep it presentable.

Around this time, new technology came out for deaf people called telecommunications for the deaf. It was used by many deaf people, but I did not have the money to have an installation by British Telecom. My grandmother offered to pay £160 for the phone line to be installed at my house. Text phone, sometimes called Minicom, is similar to a standard telephone. It plugs into your socket at home and the display lets you type and read conversations.

She phoned Social Services to ask for Textphone but the social worker refused. My grandmother was furious. She rang them several times and eventually they agreed to let me have one. It looked very much like a typewriter on which I could type a message to another Textphone so another deaf person could read it or if I wanted to get in touch with hearing people I would have to use a special number to connect to RNID, the Royal National Institution for the Deaf. Someone would read my message and call the hearing person on the other end, then type out what the hearing person said. But it is more expensive to use than a normal phone, and how would I know if someone had called me?

Again you would have to get in touch with the social worker to send an electrician to come to your house, put in a box and install the textphone. When someone called, the lights in my house would turn on and off quickly, and I would then know that I was receiving a message. I would then type 'Hello' and have a conversation with another deaf person.

The only problem I had was that the lights would only work downstairs, not upstairs. The social worker (a different one this time) knew I was deaf and if I was upstairs I would miss the call, also if I was asleep. I found out that other deaf people's homes did have every room light working when the phone rang, and the doorbell too. If I was upstairs I would miss that. My grandmother phoned them for me and explained that it was stupid just to have the downstairs light working.

I have never liked social workers, because I have always felt that they were not there to help me but to save money.

Philip and Jamie went to the nursery, which was within the Catholic primary school at Sacred Heart, and they continued to go to school there at the same area near the nursery. I believed that they would receive the best education there. We all attended mass every Sunday and sometimes we would attend with the school pupils at the church. Once a month at the deaf mass the priest used sign language. Sometimes Philip would be an altar boy.

I had never missed their school plays or parents' evenings and I continued to do so at the secondary school. When Philip left the school he got five GCSEs (Maths D, English D, PE C, Geography F, Science D). He hated going to school and never liked the people there, and he could not wait to leave. He decided to go to a college of performance art to do drama, but didn't enjoy it. He then did several jobs and worked at a pizza shop, and one day he came home from the Job Centre and said he had got a new job, at Butlins at Minehead – so far away!

He was nineteen years old with no money, and he was going to be working in the kitchen serving fish and chips! I waved him off at the bus station, very upset. Jamie said to me he thought it was time I got a mobile phone, but I was not sure if I would be able to use it. Jamie told me to buy one and he would show me how to use it to text Philip. I was then able to text Philip any time. He would text me saying he did not like working there as some people were taking drugs and his bedroom was flooded, but the managers did not care. In the end he came home that weekend and never went back! Thank God for mobile phones. That was my first ever mobile phone at the age of 40 years old!

Philip's next job was at Garland Call Centre and he then left to work for British Gas, then there was a car wash job and a job at the Gazette. He was not happy there, so he decided to be a car salesman like Jamie. In the end he decided to go back to the Gazette, where he now has a permanent job as manager of the newspaper office.

When Jamie left school he did well, with GCSE Drama D, English Speaking B, English Language C, English Literature D, Maths D, Geography D, Science D. he was always interested in joinery and he started to do an apprenticeship at Carillion to learn joinery. When he finished his apprenticeship at 18 he worked for an agency for a year and half, but he was always in and out of jobs. He got a bit fed up, so he left and worked in a call centre for Virgin for five months. He was not happy working there either. He got NVQ 1,2,3, in vehicle sales, which equates to a Diploma. He went to work for Reg Vardy/Evans Halshaw and still works there today.

When my sons both started working I got the most wonderful surprise at Christmas - a new automatic washing machine! That was a luxury for me. I could vacuum and dust while the clothes were being washed, all at the same time, and I didn't have to use rubber gloves any more! I never knew how much easier it would be just put in the clothes in, then take them out and hang them on the line.

My mother and father at their wedding in 1956

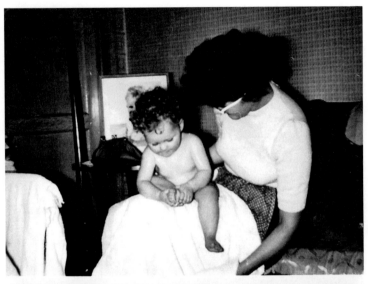

With my mother, aged nine months

Aged three, with my brother Stephen (one year old)

5 Aged eight (centre) with brothers Stephen (six) and David (five)

Aged eight

My little sister Jill, aged six

The pupils of Boston Spa School

The nuns of Boston Spa School

With my friend Joan (right) in 1975

With Joan (right), in York, 1976

My elder son Philip,
aged seven months

My younger son Jamie,
aged eight months

Philip and Jamie, 1986

Philip and Jamie, 1991

Philip and Jamie, 1993

With Jill and David at David's wedding

CHAPTER FIVE

Defeating depression

I did wonder when I was going to get a letter from Michael, as it had been 19 years since we had last seen him and I would have to be prepared for him to want his money from the house and to have the house sold and divide the money between us as Jamie turned 17, but I received nothing. Then in 2008 I received a letter from a solicitor on behalf of Michael instructing me to sell the house. I got very upset as I was only working part time. I had to rely on my sons to make phone calls and arrange for a solicitor and go with me to see the solicitor on their days off. I got some photos taken of the rooms in the house to take to the solicitors to prove that I had spent a lot of money on the house, redecorating every room, having the central heating put in and a new boiler, plus new doors and a new bathroom. I had letters coming and going to the solicitors. However we did come to an agreement on the price of the house. I then had to get a mortgage, so I had to ask Jamie on his day off work to go to see a financial adviser. Fortunately we were able to get a mortgage and pay Michael off. That meant we all were finally free of him. We have not seen or heard from him since then.

I started to eat more unhealthy food, like fish and chips or Chinese takeaways. I would buy a box of chocolates and hide it because I wanted to eat them all myself – I would eat the lot in one night, and very soon I put on a lot of weight. I couldn't understand why – I didn't seem to care, just carried on eating, and I didn't have a period for a long time. I would always feel tired, but never had any sleep. I would lie awake in bed.

It took me a long time to realize that I had depression. I think it was due to the fact that I was at home looking after my son's and my own daily life with little money and little social life. I was depressed for about seven years and wanted to go to the doctors but kept putting it off, as I knew communication would be difficult. I found food and chocolate comforting. It took me a while to buck up the courage and go to consult Dr Smith (I had been told his son was deaf) by writing it down on paper. He give me low dosage anti-depression tablets. I did later go to see him again to ask if I could get counselling, but he refused.

I really wanted to do something with my life, and when I learned that other deaf people were teaching hearing people sign language I was very interested. However I felt I was too fat and ugly to do that, but I did not really know who to ask about it. I just happened to mention it to this man called Keith Williams who worked at the deaf club as advocated for the deaf people. He was deaf himself, and he was helpful and advised me to go to college and do curriculum training. I thought that if I went to college to be a teacher and got a job teaching it would motivate me to go out of the house more.

I decided to do regular exercise and take up running, and I soon learned to change the way I ate. I bought myself a book about foods, because I knew I could not attend the Weight Watch class as I would not be able to follow the teacher. I saw a Weightwatchers book which I found simple to follow with interesting and different foods. I could have as much fruit and vegetables as I liked, and there were plenty of pictures, which helped me to understand better and only cost £7 in a sale. I still use it today!

Slowly I started to lose weight and my clothes were getting too big on me to wear. Eventually I lost three stones in weight and was more motivated to look for work. I had realized that taking antidepressant pills does not help the problem. I decided to come off them slowly. For seven years I felt like that – who could I go and ask for help? I found it difficult to tell someone. That was the darkest place I have ever entered, and I made sure I would never be in that dark place like that again.

Philip developed asthma as well as Jamie. I did ask for both of them to be treated at the same hospital and continued every three months rather than every year. When Jamie started at the Catholic school full time I would give him his nebulizer, which was the one where I had to pump the air with my foot to release the air, in the morning before school and then go back to pick him up from school, bring him home to give him his lunch and recharge it again for the afternoon. So for a year I had to make three return trips to school five days a week.

I was not happy with the next-door neighbour because they got themselves a Doberman, the most ugly and aggressive dog I have ever come across. They made a shed in the yard for the dog to sleep in and he would walk around in circles all day. They never took him out for a walk, and he would poo in the yard. I had to be careful every time I opened the curtains in the boys' bedroom in case the dog barked. It continually barked in an aggressive way day and night and early in the morning, and I didn't sleep very well for worry that Philip and Jamie would not be able to sleep. I absolutely hated that dog – I have never liked dogs anyway.

One time I was looking over at their yard when the son purposely encouraged it to bark at the window. Can you imagine my rage? I quickly opened the net curtains and gave the man a dirty look – he looked shocked when he saw me! I assume he thought it was my boys. I wanted to something about it, but how was I to go about doing that? I am sure they didn't care because they knew I would not be able to hear that dog, and my boys were suffering.

I did go to the neighbour who lived on the other side of them about the dog, because I knew she worked nights and slept through the day. I asked if the dog was bothering her and she said no, he was fine! We put up with that for five years, till one day a new neighbour moved in at the near end of the street. They'd only been there a week when they rang my door bell. At the door were two girls in their early 20s. They asked me if I would mind keeping the dog quiet! I quickly said 'I don't have a dog, it's them next door,' and pointed out the house to them. Within a week that dog disappeared – forever!

I believe I was taken advantage of because of my disabilities. These were the same people who said to me that they did not have phone when I asked them to call the police. I was so relieved when the dog went and even happier when they moved away! Now we have a nicer neighbour and no dog. The new neighbour, Mark, even told us when he was planning to have a party and promised to keep it quiet, which he did.

I never felt comfortable letting my boys play outside in the street. I would have to keep an eye out of the window all the time to make sure they were safe, because I could not hear anything if something did happen. One day after tea they went outside to play for about ten minutes after tea. I was in the kitchen washing up when a neighbour came to my house to tell me something had happened. She quickly took me around the corner and Philip came running to me in a shocked state to say Jamie had been hit by a car!

I ran out of the house so fast and found Jamie on the ground. I quickly picked him up. We were all in shock and I did not understand what I was being told. My neighbour explained that the man wanted to take us to hospital. I went home to lock the door and we all went in his car, and I remember none of us said a word. I never saw that man again. He was the one who had knocked Jamie over.

After being checked over by the doctor at the hospital we were told that thankfully Jamie was fine and only had bruises on his legs.

About two or three days later police officers came to our house, saying the accident had been reported. I was surprised, because I had not told them about it. I kept asking them to speak slowly, as I was not able to understand some things. Philip said the man who had hit Jamie had reported himself to the police. To this day I have never known the man's name.

The church I attended asked if we would like to go as pilgrims to Lourdes, where sick and disabled people go every year to stay for a week of prayers. They asked us if we would like to go, all expenses paid, and I agreed to go to pray for my sons' health. We stayed in a hotel overlooking the river. It was the first time on a plane for us, and the weather was beautiful all that week. We met wonderful people who were so willing to help us – it was a different world. My mother came with us. I have since been five times, sometimes with friends and with my mother twice.

I wanted my boys to do well in school and never missed attending parents' evenings to discuss their schoolwork and any school plays they were in. My father came along for support and was interested in how they were doing. When they were at secondary school I was thinking about going back to work and took a few courses at college for computer operating, but found them difficult and considered doing a teaching job with British Sign Language. As Keith Williams advised me, I decided I would go to college to gain Level Three NVQ teaching certificates and to build profiles. I found it difficult, but I was pleased to pass and did an assessment for Level Two British Sign Language at Durham University – I passed that too. I couldn't wait to start to teach hearing people how to learn British Sign Language!

When I was at Kirby College for my NVQ teacher certificates, I would go one evening a week. The communicator for British Sign Language would arrived in the classroom and introduce herself to me and when the lecturer started to speak the communicator was lost! She couldn't keep up with what the lecturer was saying. I realized that she was not qualified to do that job. For the whole evening I did not learn a thing. I got in touch with the communicator support department manager by using textphone and asked for another communicator, but the following week I arrived college to find there was no communicator at all. I had to go home as there was no point in staying.

For the third week at college the person in charge of organizing communicators was there with the same lady I had made my complaints about. She had to interpret my complaints to the manager! I had to say she was useless and I was lost in the classroom for her to translate. I knew the man used to be a gas fixer and I told him he should stick to that job! I was angry, as he could not understand British Sign Language himself. How he got that job is beyond me.

The fifth time I arrived at college I finally got someone who was a little bit better, but only because that communicator had had some experience with deaf people. I needed to be able to understand and learn to create a profile for my qualifications for my future as a teacher. I would have preferred a registered qualified interpreter NVQ level six, as they are excellent and very professional. College usually uses communicators because it's cheaper. Universities should use highly-qualified interpreters.

I was offered one evening a week teaching at the deaf club, which was only ten minutes' walk from my house - very handy. Philip and Jamie were able to look after themselves for two hours now - Jamie was almost 15 years old. Sometimes I could keep an eye on them at the park opposite the deaf club upstairs where I was working, and I could see them playing football.

The very first evening going to work I was very excited and nervous at the same time, but looking forward to it. Fifteen students arrived and sat around in a half circle and my co-ordinator introduced me to all the students, telling them I was deaf and giving a brief explanation about the course, which was to take 30 weeks, with exams at the end of the term. Then she left. There I was starting to teach fifteen students British Sign Language and I had no idea what I was going to be paid!

Firstly I would have flip charts. I would write 'Hello' using my right hand with palm facing toward the students and going around in small circles. Then all the students did the same, all at the same time. Then I would have them do it one by one, then for the next one I would write 'How are you?' I would then show them first by putting both my hands on my chest and slowly moving out with my hands away to the right hand shape and mouth movement at the same time. I had to be careful as there are many basic hand shapes, for example flat hand, open hand, clawed hand, fist, closed hand, bent hand, cupped hand and so on. There's also pointing, movement and facial expressions to show emotions like angry, excited, jealous, sorry and so on.

I would teach and show the alphabet to each student first, then they would watch me, then copy me. Once I had made sure everyone understood clearly, I would hand out copy alphabet sheets and the students would learn how to finger-spell their names. By the end of the class each student should be able to sign hello and then finger-spell their names.

During my time teaching, my coordinator-manager asked me if I would like to go for an interview. I agreed, in the end. The interviews were delayed and I ended up being interviewed at the same time as another woman. We sat down and he took out a pen and paper and asked me what I did at work, and I told him. The other lady said 'I work in prison and teach'. Then he asked me about the Mayor, and I remembered a poster I had been looking at while I was waiting and said that the Mayor considered our health and well-being. I also said he had been to the deaf centre a few times meeting with deaf people, and there were many photographs all around the walls of the Mayor with deaf people who had done well with their exams on computer courses. He was delighted with me for mentioning that, and while I was answering his questions he was writing everything down

The other woman became quite annoyed, as he seemed to be asking me more questions about the Mayor than my job. I was really glad that I had seen that poster!

When I saw my coordinator at work the following week and I told her all about it she could not believe it and could not understand why is was important that I had to answer these questions. I found the whole thing unbelievable. The Mayor was more important to them than learning about my job! In fact the Mayor used to be a policeman and had been sacked from his job for making deals with a drug dealer – and today he still is Mayor!

CHAPTER SIX

Into the employment jungle

In 2004 they introduced Job Seekers' Allowance. I was on income support and could not understand why I received a letter to attend the Job Centre and see a Disability Employment Adviser. I was confused as we could not communicate because I didn't have an interpreter, and the DEA did not know what to do. I wrote down on a piece of paper that I was working and was told that I might have more classes. He shook his head as if to say I could not. I was told to come again in two weeks' time. At the next appointment he wrote a note saying I would have a different Disability Employment Adviser next time, pointing at a woman who was sitting at her desk. This woman could sign a little, but I never got an interpreter while I was with her. She too shook her head as if to say 'well you can't work'.

I was advised to see someone from the Citizen's Advice Bureau, so I made an appointment there. They arranged for an interpreter and I explain that the DEA was not helping me to find work or advising me about my teaching job. They arranged for me to attend the CAB again, and they explained that because

I was on Incapacity Benefit because of my disabilities and depression, I would have to write to the doctor to agree that the doctor would be happy to help me, which meant changing benefit to replacing therapeutic rules with new permitted work rules that would enable me to work and claim job seekers' allowance. So I was allowed to work.

I explained what had happened to my mother, who was pleased for me and said she would go with me. When I went along with my mother she explained the situation to Dr Smith, but he flatly refused to write a letter to allow me to work or confirm that I was disabled, because he said there was nothing wrong with me. I could not believe I had been refused. I got very upset.

We decided to go to the CAB again, and when we arrived there my mother explained what had happened at the surgery with Dr Smith. The solicitor could not believe that the doctor had refused my request and was very angry. She said the doctor had no right to refuse and she would write him a letter.

Then to my surprise I received a letter from Dr Smith which said: 'This patient of mine, who is profoundly deaf, carries out part-time work on two evenings per week in order to teach sign language. This work has a mainly therapeutic element to her in that she gains benefit from passing on skills to others, which she knows from personal experience will benefit the deaf community as a whole. I understand that this is paid work and that it is likely to prevent her from being able to claim full benefits for her own disability. I would be grateful if the obvious practical therapeutic benefits of her part-time work could be taken into consideration. Yours sincerely, Dr R Smith.'

YES! I had to read the letter twice! That letter confirmed that I was disabled and needed the job for therapeutic reasons which would help my mental health. I was very pleased, although I was warned that I might have to pay £13 for the letter. However I never did receive a bill.

I then went back to see the Disability Employment Adviser. I was about to explain about therapeutic permitted work and the B7 form, but I had not finished saying what I wanted to say when she quickly said 'Oh yes, this is form B7'. She got up and went over to a cupboard with piles of different forms and gave me a form B7. The whole time I had been attending the Job Centre, that cupboard behind her had held those B7 forms, and she had never mentioned them.

So what is the Disability Employment Adviser's job? It was so important for me as a deaf person to be working and seeking employment at the same time, to be able to show something on my CV and to show the employers that I was capable of full-time employment. It had made me realise that it was not difficult for the Disability Employment Adviser to behave like that, because nothing was black and white and nothing was ever written down on paper.

I was then pleased to be given three more classes. I continued to enjoy them and was always looking forward to them. Teaching enabled me to save up a bit of money, and I was hoping to get full-time employment. I am not sure why, but the Disability Employment Adviser advised me to go to disabled forums to look for work with other people with different disabilities on Thursdays, and when I went I was told to look in the newspaper for jobs and look for work on the computer – not very much help to me really.

I never went back to that place again because I felt I was not getting any help or gaining anything by going there. I told the Disability Employment Adviser that the disabled forum was not suitable for me and was not helping me, and I thought it was a waste of time for me to keeping going. She did not know what to say – she just said 'I was a bit worried about that'.

About two weeks later she told me that there was a job at Rede House, which was being opened up for business. It was office work without the telephone, and training would be given for eight weeks. I said I was interested in working in an office as I had done it before. She gave me an application form, but there was no advice or extra help with it. I need help with filling in the application form because it needed to be accurate. I asked my sister for help with it.

On the day of attending the interview I made a lot of effort and looked very smart, but I was excited and nervous at the same time. I must have been the first candidate at nine o'clock, and I couldn't believe what I was seeing. That interpreter was more like a communicator. She said she was just learning to do level three British Sign Language, yet I needed a level six NVQ registered interpreter! But what could I do? Nothing – the interview was just five minutes away. I just had to go ahead with the interview.

The two employers both gave me that look as if they had never seen a deaf person before. I felt the interview went well however, because I was able to answer the questions. But I still felt uncomfortable with that interpreter and I certainly was not well pleased with her because she said quite a few times, 'sorry, I don't understand'. I would have to repeat it, or she would say to the employee, 'Can you say that clearly?' or ask me what I was trying to say, which is totally unacceptable.

I had to wait for a month before I received a letter to say I had not got the job. I was very upset and sick at the thought of returning to the Job Centre. I told the Disability Employment Adviser that she was wrong to book an interpreter who was still learning for an interview, and she did not know what to say. Then I asked her to call them and ask why I had not got the job. She didn't really want to call them, but she did, and they told her that the interpreter was not very good – so I had not got the job because of the interpreter!

I had said during the interview that I would need an interpreter for eight weeks' training. It was within my rights to ask this, under the Disability Discrimination Act. She did not know what to do or say, so she did nothing. She made no attempt to persuade the employers that I was capable of doing the job, or explain about my rights under the Act. It was obvious that she hadn't got a clue.

I could not believe it when four weeks after that interview the Disability Employment Adviser advised me to go to the open day of the same company that had refused to give me the job! I thought I would have to try again so I went along, only to find that I had to sit in a room full of people with a lady making speech for an hour using pictures on a projector. Why was I forcing myself to sit through that? Everyone was making notes and putting their hands up to ask questions. I was absolutely lost. When we looked around the offices I felt sick, because I saw the two people who had interviewed me and they did not know where to look when they saw me. I saw the computers on the desk without the telephone, which would have been perfect for me.

As I was leaving I picked up an application form on my way out - I did not stay long. Again I asked my sister to help fill in the same application form and hoped and pray for another interview, but it never came. What did the Disability Employment Adviser do? Nothing.

What was I going to do now? I thought for a long time. All I wanted to do was work in an office, but I realized that it would never happen. But what else could I do? Did the Disability Employment Adviser advise me? Certainly not!

I thought I would like to be a teaching assistant at a mainstream school, but I didn't like the thought of going back to college yet again. I knew the communicators were only qualified Level Two in British Sign Language and that is not good enough for me (or anyone studying in college. However, I decided to go to college yet again.

I was told I would have to do some voluntary work at school as part of my college work and to create a profile for my exams. I knew of a unit for deaf children in a mainstream school, as no deaf children now attended Beverley School. My sister found a number and I tried several times by using the minicom/textphone to ask if I could do volunteer work there, but I never got reply from the teachers or the receptionist. In the end I had to ask my sister to call them on my behalf and that was when they agreed that I could do the volunteer work.

The teacher agreed for me to come on Monday mornings. On the first morning I was taken to a classroom where there were children between five and six. No one asked me for my disclosure and barring service checks (previously CRB checks). It was only when I approached the teacher for the deaf about it after one month that she said she had forgotten. She then asked me to bring my CV and the disclosure and barring check papers. I was astounded that I was allowed to do volunteer work without anyone checking the papers on me, for these are the extremely vulnerable deaf children.

That mainstream school was a different world from my own school, and I felt it was not right for the children and the teachers for the deaf. Their sign language was very poor and I would fall asleep when the teacher was using British Sign Language because it was boring and because it was old school and the teachers were not as professional or qualified as the NVQ level six registered interpreters. I felt I had seen and learned since I had left Beverly.

While I was going to college and doing volunteer work at the school one morning a week and teaching three classes, I was also looking after my family and learning to drive. One of my former students was working in a supermarket and told me that she hated filling up shelves with tins. Unknown to me, she applied for a school job and was offered an interview at the same school where I was doing the volunteer work, as an assistant working with deaf children. Yet she had only just passed level one British Sign Language, which meant she had only learned for 30 weeks and a total of 60 hours.

I asked her how this had come about. She explained that she had filled a form in and sent it to the council and several weeks afterwards she received a phone call to ask if she would be interested in going to this particular school. When she went to meet the teacher she was asked to have a look around the school and conversed with the teacher for the deaf for about ten minutes. She told the teacher that she liked what she had seen and the teacher offered her the job. I found this astounding and felt fundamental questions needed to be asked. Did no one check her communication skills in British Sign Language?

Here I was going to college every week for three hours' study and to build a profile and doing volunteer work every Monday at the same school. But wasn't I the right person for that job? Was there another deaf teaching assistant at that school? There were two I knew of, and this one had gone from working in a supermarket to this job 25 hours a week, with no knowledge of deaf children's different degrees of deafness, no working experience with deaf children and no understanding of deaf children's behaviour.

I did set up a meeting with the head teacher to complain about it, but I don't think he understood my problem and nothing was changed. I couldn't believe it.

I did find the course difficult, but I managed to finish it and pass my exams. I applied to the council for teaching assistant positions by filling in an application which had only one sheet to fill in, but no job was offered. I felt my time had been wasted. When I did volunteer work it certainly opened my eyes. Is it working for the mainstream schools? Is there is any research into deaf children's education today? Once again I had to continue going to the Job Centre.

Then I was surprise to receive a message on my textphone from a social worker. She was asking if I would be interested in being on the panel for interviewing deaf and hearing people for jobs as social workers! I didn't hesitate. I replied to the social worker to say that I would be interested. We then arranged the day and time and when I arrived on the day I was an hour early. I met the head of the social work department and a lady who was in charge of the social workers. She asked me a few questions, and was surprised when I said we had to take different degree of deafness into account. 'Er... yes you are quite right', she said. I did not know if any of them had any experience with deaf people or if any of the hearing persons had learned British Sign Language. The only people who read the application forms were the social workers and the head of the department, who were going to be on the panel to do the interviewing.

There were four of us on the panel, two deaf people and two hearing people. We would ask two questions each of 10 applicants. The first hearing man's questions were not strong enough. After the interview we could discuss the candidate and I would write down the points he or she had earned for each question, then we would work out who had got the most points.

The next one was a hearing lady. She came in the room and smiled and sat down on the chair. The manager explained that she would be asked two questions in British Sign Language and she would have to respond in sign language. Suddenly her body language changed and she was not smiling any more. I thought, what is the matter?

I started to sign the first question and she got more and more upset. The lady next to me said to her, 'It's all right, you can take your time'. I knew straight away that she was not able to use British Sign Language and would not be the right person for the job. She said, 'I work with adults with learning disabilities and I did learn British Sign Language some time ago, but I have not worked with or met a deaf person or used British Sign Language since I passed Level two exams'.

The atmosphere in that room was awful and she was crying for quite a while. We all tried to reassure her that is was all right and she could learn sign language later. I blamed those who had invited her for the interview. I was sorry for her, but at the same time I thought that if I had seen what she had written on the application form about her experience and qualifications I probably would not have asked her for an interview.

We interviewed six more people, of whom three were deaf. We agreed that it had gone all right. We had written down points for each question and left it like that. We were to come back again next week to interview five more.

This time there were three deaf people and two hearing people. The first was a deaf man – I knew him and what he did for a living. His answers to my two questions were excellent and it carried on the same way with the rest of the questions each of us asked. When it was finished we were all very impressed and I put him at the top of the my list. He was working in a residential home for deaf adults with learning disabilities. One of the questions he put to the head of the social services was if the hours could be increased. The social services manager said maybe, in the near future.

The next interviewee was a hearing lady who was able to use British Sign Language, which was all right but not great. I found her answers poor and gave her low points. I could tell she had worked with deaf people, however. When it was finished we discussed her and agreed that she was average. The last person was a deaf man and his interview with us was not very good. I did not have to think carefully to decide who the right person for the job was – the deaf man. We all agreed.

That was a good and interesting learning experience for me and I believed more of this should be happening everywhere. Sadly it does not.

A couple of weeks later I was at the deaf centre and asked the social worker if the man we had chosen had accepted the job. She said he had not, so it had been given to the lady who I had thought was average. I was very disappointed. I was able to ask him myself when I was at the deaf centre a few months later, and he said the hours had not been enough for him.

During my time in college, I thought if I learned to drive it would help me with getting a job if I were to work further afield or working shifts. But where could I find a driving instructor with some basic knowledge of British Sign Language? I wasn't likely to find one in Yellow Pages! Philip suggested that he would ask his driving instructor if he knew someone, and luckily he did and passed me his details.

I was very nervous and excited for my first driving lesson. John, the instructor, took me somewhere very quiet and taught me by letting me watch his foot on the brakes and accelerator. He was able to use very basic signs, which helped while I was driving. He would use his hands slightly forward so I could see them. If he wanted me to turn right he would use his right hand and his left for turning left. If he wanted me to go straight ahead he would use his palm to show me, and he would keep pointing his index finger to the mirror to remind me to use it! As we were approaching a roundabout he would move his index finger in a circle and then tell me to either turn or go straight on.

It was difficult at first because not only did I have to watch his basic signs, I had to learn how to use the pedals, clutch, brakes and accelerator. John would sit in the driving seat and show me how they worked and then we would swap seats and I would use them myself to show I could learn it all. But that was not all – I had to do the theory test. For me to study the book was the most boring and the hardest thing I have ever done, and some of the words I had never heard before. It was very expensive too.

On the day of the theory test I was presented with a qualified interpreter, NVQ level six. She signed the questions and I had to type in the answer from the computer. When it was over I was very glad to be told I had passed the theory test at my first attempt. I continued learning to drive, which took me nearly a year. On the day of the test I was annoyed that the instructor did not know what to do or how to use simple basic signs. This did not help my nervousness. When he did use his hand to tell me to turn right, I did so, but he said no, not that one, the one in the end of this road!

Did I pass my driving test the first time? No I did not! I knew I would have to pay more money, and there was no instructor with basic British Sign Language. I discussed it with my driving instructor and he said he could only explain to them that I needed to understand which way they wanted me to go. This did not help me. After I had failed three times I was thinking about giving up, but decided to give it one more go. The fourth time, I passed – and it was the examiner who had failed me the first time! I was so pleased it was all over, as it had been very expensive.

Then I received a letter to confirm that the Disability Employment Adviser would no longer assist me. I was given another DEA and wondered if he would be any better qualified for the job. When I arrived to meet him, I felt he was just the same as the others. I had to face the Job Centre with the same man every two weeks with an interpreter for about a year, but then I found a job as advocate for the deaf at the fire station, advertised on the deaf club notice board. I was delighted, but I found some of the job description off-putting because it did say a quite a bit about communication with staff at the station and making phone calls, which I thought might find it difficult. However I still wanted to apply for it.

I photocopied the advertisement and took it with me to show it to the new Disability Employment Adviser. I was excited and could not wait for his help and advice, but instead he looked quite shocked. I asked about the situation with the phone calls and communicating with staff. He had not been looking for work for me – he had done nothing at all. He did not know where to look. He shrugged his shoulders and said nothing. In the end the interpreter stepped in and said I could apply for the job because I could use an 'Access To Work' interpreter who could come to my work place and give me advice, and explain what the job description meant.

I felt a bit better knowing that I could do the job. What did that Disability Employment Adviser do and say? Absolutely nothing ! He certainly was not comfortable. He quickly said 'sign here, goodbye'. I went home in a daze wondering what to do next.

I thought I had better go and see my sister Jill, even though it had been snowing heavily for several days and not many transport services were available. I knew she was very busy packing up to go to Australia, so I apologised and asked her for help with the application form. She was more than happy to help me fill it in – she is very good at doing them for me.

I went home relieved that the application form was done and I sent it immediately the next day by recorded delivery. While I was waiting to see if I would be given an interview I knew my next job would be looking for an interpreter, and I was not sure when to get one.

Then I received a call on my textphone from a fire officer, to ask which day would be best for me to attend the interview. He asked if I would like to book an interpreter of my choice. I quickly gave him her name and hoped that she would be available on the day of interview. That would save me using my time and money looking around for an interpreter. it is more expensive using the textphone than the normal phone.

CHAPTER SEVEN

'Never seen a deaf person before'

I was excited to be asked for an interview and was hoping that I would not have to attend the Job Centre any more. The job was part-time, only for eighteen hours a week, which meant that I still could teach British Sign Language on Mondays and Tuesdays. I prayed it would go well and studied the safety of everything that was needed in the home. Why didn't the Disability Employment Adviser do that for me? It was history repeating itself! He did absolutely nothing.

I was so pleased to receive a letter confirming an interview with the interpreter of my choice. I went back to see the Disabilities Adviser. I could not believe he would just sit there expecting me to say I had filled in the application forms myself and searched around for an interpreter. He was being paid by the taxpayer to help deaf people to come off benefit and go into employment.

I really wanted that job. On the day of the interview I got up very early and put on my best brown suit and boots, matching my handbag. I even went to the hairdressers to have my hair done. My son took me the 20 miles in my car. I was both nervous and excited and kept telling myself to be positive.

When I arrived the officer apologised, as I was supposed to be interviewed by three officers but one had to attend elsewhere, so only two interviewed me. But I felt it went really well and I hoped and prayed I would be asked for a second interview.

While I was waiting for the second interview I had to attend the Job Centre, and the Disability Employment Adviser asked me if I was going to be interviewed again. I could only say that I was still waiting and could not wait to leave. I was only there for five minutes.

At the second interview I wore a blue suit, and kept telling myself that I was closer to leaving the Job Centre and beginning a new life. The three fire officers were quite understanding, but I still felt I was getting the 'never seen a deaf person before' look, even though the previous person in the post had been deaf.

I felt the second interview went really well and was very pleased with myself. I had no problems with the interpreter. I kept looking for the post every day. After about two weeks a brown envelope arrived on the floor and I saw that it was from the fire station. I did not dare to open it but just kept walking around the room with it for about fifteen minutes. When I eventually opened it, my heart sank and darkness came over me. It said I had a lot of qualities and had done very well at the interview, but they could not offer me the job or offer feedback. I knew only four deaf and one hearing person had gone for the interview.

I was extremely upset for the next two weeks and could not sleep or eat very well. I had desperately been hoping for a new chapter in my life and had strongly believed that the job was suitable for a deaf person. I knew I was able to do both teaching and working as advocated for the deaf people. I could teach all the fire staff at that station with my wealth of knowledge and improve the understanding of deaf people's safety in everyday life.

I had this churning horrible and was sick in my stomach at the thought of having to go and face the Job Centre and continue seeing that same adviser.

There was a rumour going around at the deaf club that the fire station where I had had the interview had employed a hearing person with no knowledge of British Sign Language to be an advocate for the deaf. I remember at the interview I was asked several questions relating to how to help deaf people in their homes and what advice I should be giving to them to make their homes safer. I would show them around the house and teach them how to make sure doors were closed at night before going to bed, and look around for the safety fire escape. I would also have to explain twice to a deaf person who might have a learning difficulty as well, and I understood the difficulties, because these deaf people are vulnerable, so I would ensure that they would be understood correctly before I left the house.

Was I ever going to get a job? The previous person who had left the post had been deaf. How could I sleep? I never did sleep very well, because I knew I would have to continue to go to the Job Centre and I did not want to face that Disability Employment Adviser again.

When I arrived and sat down he asked if I had been looking for any more jobs, although he knew I had just been for two interviews. I said I had looked, but there was nothing suitable yet.

'Right' he said, 'I have found this one receptionist's job at the hospital 15 hours a week and you can do that job with the interpreter working and standing next to you.' He said it very aggressively. I got upset and angry. I just could not sit and say nothing, so I said 'You call yourself a Disability Employment Adviser? You are absolutely rubbish!'

He replied, 'Oh! Do you want me to get another Disability Employment Adviser for you?'

'What is the point, you are all exactly the same' I said. 'Why don't you learn British Sign Language?'

He shrugged and pointed his finger to the interpreter. I just thought enough was enough and walked out. I cried all the way home.

I thought I had better do something about it and I was thinking about making a complaint to the manager. I did not apply for the jobs he asked me to apply for. If I had applied for that receptionist job, my chance of an interview would be zero.

I dreaded seeing that man again. The next time I arrived he immediately said, 'Do you want me to give them your mobile number?'

'Who?' I said. 'I am not giving out my text number to someone I don't know, why?'

'That's the booklet' he said. He gave it to me with no explanation. 'Right, come downstairs' he said. He took me to another man at a desk on the ground floor and said, 'From now on you sign here'. Then he left.

That was it. That was the last time I saw him. Why was I told to sign on down on the ground floor and not upstairs with a Disability Employment Adviser any more, I have no idea. It meant I was not going to have anyone helping me or getting any support to seek employment.

I did look up the Working Links booklet on the internet. There was no information about supporting deaf people. I searched and searched and there was absolutely nothing.

I now had to go to the Job Centre every two weeks to sign on the ground floor. I was supposed to look on the internet, apply for jobs, write eight letters and make several phone calls. I decided to complain to the manager and get help with this from the Citizens' Advice Bureau, because I needed help with writing and because of the way I had been threatened by the Disability Employment Adviser. I thought the Citizens' Advice Bureau would be able to help with legal advice. They wrote a letter to the manager on my behalf, but I had to wait a long time before I received a letter from him saying my complaint would have to investigated, and they would then reply with the findings. Then after another long wait I finally received a letter saying that they had found that the Disability Employment Adviser was not guilty of any wrongdoing. I could not sleep, and felt so frustrated that nothing had been done to solve my problem. It seemed that no one took the Disability Discrimination Act as relevant to me.

I received a letter with the date to attend the 'working link' (work programmed) and it did not mention providing an interpreter. When I arrived and no interpreter was present, I waited and waited. Eventually a lady came over and I gave her the letter of appointment. I was to attend for three hours. She looked at the paper and said 'Right, come upstairs'. I was taken to a room full of hearing people, where someone was supposed to give us all a speech and teach us how to get into employment. But because there was no interpreter, he said I couldn't stay and I was invited to go home.

I could see that he was not capable and did not have a clue about deaf people. When he tried to interpret a sign in a mocking way, I found it insulting. I knew straightaway that he had never met a deaf person. Obviously he had been given the job and I just had to go there regardless of my disabilities, but I suspect he did not have the knowledge.

A week later I received another letter to say that it was my fault because I had not given them my minicom number and did not want interpreter present. This had come from the Disability Employment Adviser – he had passed that information on to them after the last time I had seen him. But on the top of the letter they had sent me was a phone number for hearing people, and next to it was 'TEXTPHONE:' on the top of the letter – without a number!

I arrived in dismay, knowing that I would not have the right person helping me. On the day of the appointment I had to sit on a computer with the interpreter with lists of questions I had to answer relating to jobs that had nothing to do with deaf people. I was forced to answer the list of question. I just clicked 'NO' all the way through without looking at the questions, and it still look an hour! Then I went home.

Then I received another letter informing me that I had to sit with a so called 'Personal Consultant' at the Working Links. When I arrived the Personal Consultant asked for my email address. I said I would prefer a letter. He was assertive and high-handed, and this was not in a private room but out in the open space where everyone could see me using British Sign Language. I was scared and felt extremely uncomfortable. He said 'If you want me to send you a letter YOU go to college and YOU learn English, then I will send you a letter, the same as the asylum seekers and immigrants that come to this country'.

I started to get very upset, and my legs were shaking. He asked 'Do you work?' and I said yes, part-time teaching. He said 'What is the part-time job? What other jobs have you been looking for?' I got more even upset. He then pointed at the interpreter and told us both to go over to a desk and look for work on the computer. The interpreter's job is just to interpret. Who did this man think he was?

I said no, I could do that at home. He then said he was going to call the manager and shouted for the manager, who came over and asked what the problem was. He told the manager what had been going on and what he thought of me and said I refused to look on the computer and only worked part time. The manager looked at me and said he hadn't got a clue about deaf people and had never met one before!

He put his hand out to shake mine, but I refused. I was still shaking and extremely upset. I could not believe how I was being treated and that I had to put up with his attitude and this behaviour and aggression towards me.

The consultant then looked at the manager and said 'I think there is a deaf awareness training course somewhere, but I can't remember'. I didn't think I could put up with it and I told the manager I wanted make a complaint. He said he would give me a name and address so I could write to them, but I said, 'No thank you, I want to see the manager face to face with the interpreter.'

'Oh right, I'll arrange an appointment for you' he said. He could not understand why I wanted to come to the office and tell the manager personally rather than writing a letter.

I went home shaking and felt physically sick. I could not face the thought of having to sit down with this person, who wasn't qualified or trained to help deaf people, week in week out, but I had to go or I would get no money for a month.

I next received a letter from the Working Links Performance Manager. She wrote, 'We have searched for you and we would recommend you to go to the Work Deaf Centre which is an organization which is available around your area and I have passed this information to your Personal Consultant'. I already worked at the deaf centre! How pathetic! What were they trying to do? Trying to show that they knew what they were doing or doing something about it? I'm sure they thought they had better write something, so they sent me that pathetic letter.

I arrived to see the performance manager upstairs with the interpreter and was taken into a large empty room. Again the performance manager gave me the 'never seen a deaf person before' look. I could see that she was uncomfortable with me using British Sign Language. I told her that her letter was only fir for the bin! She did not know where to look. Then I asked her what a textphone was. She pointed at an ordinary phone. Then I showed her the letter I had received which carried the heading 'TEXTPHONE' and had no number with it. She said they would look into it.

I then explained why I could not sit with that adviser and felt he was not qualified to be a 'personal consultant' for deaf people. She said she would have a word with him. I said, 'Have a word with him? Is this a joke? Don't you have someone else who has experience with deaf people and can use sign language and who has had deaf awareness training?' I also said that I felt uncomfortable sitting where everyone could see me with the interpreter using British Sign Language, and somewhere more private would be better. She was unable to answer, and quickly give me a leaflet about the customer complaints process. That was it. I was still going to the Job Centre with lists of jobs I had to apply for and to the Working Links the following week.

At my next appointment I was faced with the same personal consultant! I couldn't believe it after the way I had been treated. Didn't the performance manager listen to anything I had said at the meeting? I straight away said I wanted to see the manager. The consultant was not pleased. Then the manager came over and said we could all sit and discuss it somewhere private. I said no, I wanted a private word with the manager on his own with the interpreter. The manager found a private room and I told him that the consultant had no respect for my language. I said I wanted to complain and showed him the leaflet. He agreed to arrange for me to make a second-level of complaint to another manager, this time the regional Business Support Manager, with the interpreter.

I arrived in the same room where I had had the first meeting with the performance manager, and noticed a carrier, a printer and computer on the table. I suspected she had done some work on it before I arrived. She said she had got another person to work with me to replace the other man, but before she went to fetch him the Business Support Manager wanted to tell me that the work programme had had some success. She tried to tell me that Working Links had made a success of helping a deaf lady into employment – she had a piece of paper about it. How pathetic! She then said that she had a replacement to help me, and I said I had several questions to ask her. I had written twenty questions. She asked me to give the papers to her so she could consult other member of staff, and I said no. She was not pleased.

She then went to fetch the lady and introduced her to me. I said to her, 'I would like to work in an office but I am unable to use the phone, would you ensure that I got a textphone or minicom to be provided within the working environment?' She could not give me an answer! I then asked another question: 'Do you understand why it is important that I go for interview with an NVQ level six interpreter?' She looked puzzled and again was unable to answer. At that point I knew she hadn't got a bloody clue. Finally I said, 'Can you explain to me how we should break down the barriers and challenges deaf people have to face?' She couldn't answer that one either.

Then the Support Manager asked her to leave the room. I'm sure she knew I was right and she did not want me to carry on asking questions. I then told her I was not satisfied with the outcome of the meeting and that she was not the right person for me. I explained that it was all about the employer making a 'reasonable adjustment' that would get me into employment, without it costing them a lot of money, so that I could work just like everyone else.

She looked at me, speechless. Then she got annoyed with me and I told her I wanted to carry on to the third level of complaint listed on the leaflet and she said coldly, 'If you want to carry on complaining to the third level I will stop your money, but I will keep checking that you are getting the right help and we will do something about the textphone. We are getting an engineer to put in a new telephone line'. She blamed the network for not having textphone set up.

I never did put in for that third level of complaint. I had to carry on going fortnightly with the woman. It made me physically ill to keep going to that horrible place knowing full well that I was never going to get the right help or knowledge from the Personal Consultant. She was actually a performance manager! She said my CV was very good, although actually it was rubbish. She said she would send it to every office around the area and they would see if there was any response. She was trying to be friendly, and saying she would like to learn British Sign Language. I did not offer any information, although that week was Deaf Awareness Week and there was an offer of free one-hour courses in British Sign Language.

The woman said she and other people were worried about their jobs. I couldn't have cared less, to be honest. Overall I only attended for a few months. And I never got a response from any of the companies she sent my CV to.

I did receive a letter from the Job Centre with an appointment there at 4.10 pm, although my normal time was 11 am. The lady on reception told me to go away and come back at 4.10 pm because I was ten minutes early. When I returned there was no interpreter again and the lady at the desk asked if I could lip read!

I immediately asked to see the manager. She went to fetch him and he escorted me to a private room with paper and pen. I wrote that I did not have an interpreter. He looked at my ears and wrote 'Do you wear a hearing aid?'

I was astonished, and have never felt so insulted. I asked him on the paper why no interpreter had been booked. He looked at the paper, then looked at me and wrote 'can you use British Sign Language? He wrote 'Wait here, I can get you one, I will book you another appointment. Do you want your bus fares?' I could not wait to get out of that place.

A couple of months later another work programme was set up called Avatar. I had to attend, though I wanted to kill myself. I really didn't want to go through all that again. When I arrived the lady asked me to fill in a form that had nothing to do with deaf people, but I had to answer those questions whether I liked it or not. I went through putting 'NO' all the way through. When it was finished I asked her what British Sign Language was and her face went bright red. I then asked, 'Have you received any specific training regarding the barriers people with hearing difficulties face?' She replied 'No'. I asked another question: 'Do you have any general deaf disability awareness training to access specialist help Access to Work for deaf people?' The response was again no. I asked, 'Have you received any training within the deaf organizations?' She said 'Yes, Royal Institution for the Deaf'. I told her, 'It's now called Action for Hearing Loss.' She replied, 'Oh really?'

She got annoyed and uncomfortable with the conversation and said she was not going to answer any more of my questions. She went to fetch the manager, who came into the room with paper and pen. I asked if his staff had had any training for deaf people and he said, 'We have had training courses for dealing with people with different disabilities'. I said DEAF people, and he repeated it I told him that was not good enough. He tried to reassure me by telling me he had two deaf friends, but he could not use sign language himself. I said 'What does that have to do with me being here?' It was obviously not going to get any better, but I knew I would have to attend or have my money stopped for a month.

At the next appointment she gave me a list of jobs to apply for, which included 'Call centre, chemical engineer sales person, barmaid and engineer! She said they gave that list to everyone. That was my help? She gave me a piece of paper and said I had to bring it back with details of jobs I had applied for. That was it.

I did complain to the Avatar head office. My sister wrote them a letter for me and their reply was 'We have an interpreter for you, what is your problem? Equity Act 2010'. That was it. Nothing was resolved and once again I just had to carry on.

I asked the Advice Manager of the Citizen's Advice Bureau to write a letter on my behalf to the Independent Case Examiner and the Job Centre plus the Customer Experience Team about my complaint. Again I had to wait a long time to hear from them. When we finally had the meeting, the Independent Case Examiner, the Advice Manager of the CAB and I put my point across. I even showed her a letter I had received from the customer services people admitting that the Disability Employment Adviser had not done any specific training in how to deal with or help deaf people wanting to get off benefit into employment. She certainly did not like that one bit, and looked very annoyed with me. I told her how I was feeling and how it was affecting me physically and emotionally and the way I had been threatened and had felt physically sick, and could not carry on facing the work programme or the Job

Centre without anybody be able to help me at all. She said 'If you feel sick about coming here don't bother, you don't have to, you know'. Goodbye. That was it.

A week later I had to attend the Job Centre again. I struggled looking for the right job for me so I wrote them down. When I arrived with my list of jobs the lady asked me why I had not looked for work or got a job. I said I needed help and found it difficult to get suitable jobs, and tried to explain. She said 'Right, no money for you, goodbye'. I received no money for a month.

I now had suicidal thoughts, and even thought of looking on the internet to see how many tablets I would have to take. I made an appointment at the doctors. I wanted to go onto another benefit called Employment Support Allowance, which would mean I would have to give up working as a teacher teaching British Sign Language and claim Employment Support Allowance (ESA) so I would not have to attend the Job Centre any more (there are two kinds of Employment Support Allowance). I did not want to do that, but I felt I did not have a choice. I knew I could not stay long at the doctors as my son came with me on his lunch hour from work and he explained how I was feeling and how I had been treated and was not receiving any help or support. The doctor didn't seem to understand how it was affecting me and said 'There is nothing wrong with you'. She advised me to go next door to see a lady in the Job Centre! I just wanted to die.

When we saw the woman at the Job Centre again my son again explained, but she just looked on the internet and said there were no jobs for me. She said she had learned sign language 10 years ago! My son explained about the money being stopped and she said I could appeal and gave me a leaflet to fill in. So going to the doctors was a waste of our time.

The thought of keeping on going to the Job Centre was just killing me. I went back to the Citizen's Advice bureau to fight to have my money back, and I did get it back, about a month later.

I feel all these people have just got away with it. I strongly believed it was wrong, because of the Disability Discrimination Act. I asked for help from the Citizen's Advice Bureau with a solicitor working with them, but they could not help because they only have trained solicitors who can only give 15 minutes. I thought, what am I going to do? Should I contact the social worker for the deaf? I did not want to, but I did not have any choice.

I went to the deaf club and saw the woman who had got the office job because the other deaf person had turned it down. Her British Sign Language was not excellent, just all right, while the other social worker was absolutely useless. When I went to the deaf club I took all the letters I had received from the Citizens' Advice Bureau and Job Centre and told her of my situation. I asked her if she could call a few solicitors for me as I wanted to sue the Government. She said I could come to the deaf centre or the office where she worked and I would have to fill in some more forms . These were for the Government to make checks on how many people the social workers were working with. Why doesn't the Government check how many social workers can use level three British Sign Language and have deaf awareness training and knowledge of different degrees of deafness?

She made four calls to solicitors, but they all said they were not licensed. One of them even said we should get in touch with the welfare officers. The social worker did say she would have to be careful not to make too many phone calls, as it would cost too much money and the manager would not like it. I was beginning to realise that I would not be eligible for legal aid. The social worker did not tell me that, I had to learn it myself. Again I wondered what I was going to do. I felt so alone in the world and tried to keep telling myself not to give up.

I looked on the internet and found the Royal Association for the deaf. The solicitor himself was deaf. I hoped it would be a help as a deaf solicitor would have a greater understanding of what I was going through. I made an appointment on Skype, which I was using for the first time. I had to go out and buy a camera to put it on top of my computer and we would communicate through using British Sign Language. The only advice he gave me was that it had to be within the last six months. That was it, and it lasted less than 30 minutes. However I sent him all the papers the next day.

While I was waiting to hear from the solicitor I told the social worker I could not carry on going to the Job Centre. She said she would come with me to see the manager, but I wondered if it would make difference. I emailed her my National Insurance number. She was supposed to make an appointment with the manager at the Job Centre and get back to me with the date of an appointment for all of us to go together, but I never got a reply.

I got more distressed and could not sleep very well. I waited for three weeks and went back to the deaf club to see the social worker. The other social worker told me she was off sick, so that never happened and I never saw her again. While I was waiting to hear from the solicitor I received by email from the EASS, Equality Advisory and Support Service, which offered an action plan with a view to resolving my issues informally without the stress of going to court or a tribunal.

Beth, my son's girlfriend, rang them on my behalf and they explained that I would need to have a meeting with the manager and then get back to them with the outcome of the meeting in writing. I then asked my sister to type a letter and send it to the manager at the Job Centre, explaining about the EASS. I had to wait for over two weeks. In the end my sister went to the Job Centre and handed in the letter. A few days later I got a letter of an appointment to see the manager (the same one who had looked at my ears). I was assertive when I put my points across and listed the problems and I even told him about the Disability Employment Adviser. He said my problem was dated and that I could not have a Disability Employment Adviser when I was in a work programme. So that was a waste of time once again.

I didn't get a reply from my solicitor for ages, and only then because the Equality Advisory and Support Service got in touch with my solicitor. He then sent me an email to ask how the meeting went. When I emailed back I waited for almost a year to hear from the solicitor. I was getting very stressed and frustrated and unable to sleep. In the end I decided to send several emails to the solicitor, because I still had to attend the Job Centre and the manager I was meeting with was there watching me to make sure that interpreter was present every time I attended. Only because of the Equity Act 2010 and the EASS had I had an interpreter present when I went with my sister. All I got was an automatic response to say he was out of the office, or another time because he was on holiday or ill. I did not think he was capable of doing his job probably and was not professional. I then sent him another email to say that I wanted to make a complaint to his manager. He was quick in replying and was very apologetic. He agreed that he had been neglecting me and promised to look into it and send me a form to fill in for legal aid for the deaf, which I got next day. I filled it in straight away and posted it, then sent recorded delivery.

I waited and waited for a response. In the end I got fed up and emailed a complaint letter straight to his manager. She promised to look into it and a few days later she emailed to apologize and admit that I was right. She gave me the name of a man who might be able to help on video which I could watch in British Sign Language. I did so, but the after the first few words I lost interested and turned it off. That was it - I never got any help from them.

I don't seem to have any rights. There isn't any law. Where was my voice? I didn't have one! To this day everyone has got away with it. To the people in the Job Centre, it's just another day in the office. In my opinion they are all uneducated, untrained, unlearned, unqualified, unintelligent, inexperienced and ignorant.

Remember that lady at the careers office? The Government claimed, 'We have backed schemes that can help while raising awareness for initiatives and challenging stereotypes about people with disabilities to ensure that everyone has a fair chance of working'. The government also claimed that a Disability Employment Adviser can help you find job or gain new skills. They can also refer you to a specialist work psychologist or carry out employment assessment, asking about your skills and experiences. I have never had any of that. I don't think they are capable of offering the help I so desperately needed.

CHAPTER EIGHT

Adventures away from home

After I had had my flashing alarm clock for some time, the wires at the back became loose. I knew I would have to return it to the social worker and ask for a replacement. I was not very happy about doing this but I needed it for work on Tuesday mornings. I walked into the deaf centre and met the manager of the social workers for the deaf for the first time and gave her the clock and said it was broken and I needed it for work. I showed her where the wires were loose and she said to leave it with her and she would get in touch when a new one arrived. A week later I received a letter to say that she would be visiting me to bring it (I did not want her to visit me at my house – I wanted to go back to the deaf centre to pick it up myself, which would only have taken me five minutes). She came in and said I had a nice house and told me a bit about her family life. To be honest I was not interested. Then she gave me a thick form for me to fill in. I asked her where my alarm clock was and she said 'I am not here for that'. I said 'Yes you are' and showed her the letter. She did not know what to say.

As I was about to fill in the form she took it from me and said she would do it for me as it was too long and difficult for me to fill in. I immediately disliked her so much that when it was finished I couldn't wait for her to leave. I then said I would go to pick up the clock myself next week at the deaf centre. That's what I did, and I never saw her again. To be honest I don't think she was doing her job properly.

I had continued to keep in touch with my friend Joan over the years by writing letters. She had got married, had two daughters and then divorced. I briefly met her father when we went for a drink one afternoon at a pub. He was ill with cancer at that time and she was looking after him. She would do his weekly food shopping for him every Friday and bring it to his flat. In the end he was taken to hospital for an operation, but he died from a weak heart.

Her brother Kieran was living in Australia. One night when he had been out drinking he went to the cashpoint, and on the way back fell and slipped on to the railway line and was killed by a train. Joan and her sisters believe he was robbed and pushed on to the track. They were not even given a chance to go to his funeral as his wife would not delay it to give them a chance to get there. My heart went out to poor Joan. I have two brothers myself and I don't know what I would do if that happened to me.

We stopped writing to each other and instead started to use the mobile phone and the internet on MSN. Joan asked me if I would be interested in going to the reunion in Manchester, where I could stay at her house for the weekend. I thought it would be a good opportunity to see her and everyone else from

St John's school Boston Spa. I went to the railway station with pen and paper to ask the lady to book a train and made sure I got a train straight from where I lived to Manchester without having to change. I also had to make sure I sat facing the digital display in the carriage as I couldn't hear the announcements. All the way I knew exactly where I was. It was wonderful to see Joan after three hours' travelling. We hugged for a quite a while.

Joan and I chatted till two in the morning! We had so much news to catch up on. She phoned my sons for me to see if they were OK. On the Friday night we went to the pub and we got a take away, then talked again into the early hours of the morning - we went to bed at three o'clock!

The dance was an opportunity for us to dress up to the nines. When we arrived at the hotel we recognised so many people from our school. It was wonderful and brought back fond memories of when we were all at school. All night we danced and drank. We ate a three-course meal and stayed up until almost four o'clock in the morning! So many of us have changed over the years! So many of us weren't getting any younger! We had fabulous time dancing and chattering for the whole weekend, and it went so quickly. Joan and I would have liked to have stayed longer!

Back at Manchester railway station I was confused by the directions I was given and could not find my platform. Fortunately I found it in the end. I kept checking my ticket to make sure it was the correct time and platform, and I kept looking down the track to make sure I got the right train. Luckily I found a seat. The train didn't leave straight away, and we had to wait for 15 minutes. It was packed, with many people standing, and I was unable to see out of the windows on my right, only the one where I was sitting. More importantly, I could not see the digital display.

The train remained packed until we arrived in Leeds. About half an hour before we arrived in York I smelled something unpleasant – there was sick all over the floor! Everyone started to get off, and I thought hang on, I paid to travel on only one train straight through. I started to panic a little. I asked the conductor and he told me it was for health and safety reasons! What was I going to do now? Was I going to have to wait around? It was no help if the loudspeaker was going to make announcements for the next train or a different platform.

While everyone was waiting I could see some cleaners arriving to clean up the sick, and while I was waiting I noticed one lady's case had a tag saying Thornaby, the station before the one where I would get off. I kept a watchful eye on that case and waited to see which train the lady would get on.

We were kept waiting for half an hour. We were finally allowed back on to the same train, and there was the lady with the case. At last I could get home.

My son Philip picked me up, but he was very quiet and only said 'Hello, did you have a good time?' When we arrived home there were two police officers there. I was shocked, but I realised why Philip had not said anything about it.

The officers spoke to me, but I told them I was deaf. Jamie was too upset to help me so there was a breakdown in communication. One of them handed me a written statement, then asked me to sign it. It was obvious they didn't have a clue how to co-operate with a deaf person. It seemed my son was upset because he had been out with his friends when he had got jumped by four boys for his mobile phone.

This all happened in one day. It was so frustrating dealing with so many communication breakdowns on the train and then with the police officers.

I received a letter about a week or so later asking me to attend court. The boys were appearing charged with stealing Jamie's phone, but because he was under sixteen I was asked to go. I asked my father to call them and explain that I was unable to attend, and they suggested that he should go in my place. I was not happy about that. My father refused. He said, 'What if I go and the young lads see me in the street, I could get attacked?' I agreed, and in the end Philip went instead.

I was not impressed. However Jamie was out with his friend before the court case and the same three lads saw him, but he ran off before anything happened, so my father was right not go. The police officers who took Jamie's statement could have sorted this out themselves and explained to us what might happen.

I continued to enjoy going for a run and kept my weight the same . I still love going for a three or four-mile run whenever I can. I do it most days, because It makes me feel good and I find it therapeutic, especially when it is warm and not too windy, but I'm still apprehensive of the dogs!

One sunny afternoon on my run, as I was coming to the path leading around the park, I noticed an Asian man under a tree holding his mobile phone and another Asian walking very slowly down the path, also using a mobile. I thought nothing of it and kept on running for about couple of minutes. Then I saw a white man who was also talking on a mobile. I thought it was strange, but dismissed it as coincidence. However on my second circuit the Asian man was alone and still under the same tree, still holding his mobile and looking at me.

I got a bit suspicious, but kept on running. The next time he was still there, but this time he was actually using his mobile phone and still looking at me. I started to feel a bit uncomfortable. The next time he was not there under the tree and I thought I was being silly. But as I went for my last run round I noticed him again, this time on the other side of the park. He was hiding behind a tree and there were two young boys playing with their bikes nearby.

The Asian man kept looking for me, then went and hid behind the tree. I did not know whether to turn around and go home or go to the fire station on the other side of the park to ask them to call the police, but I decided to keep on running as fast as I could as I was about to finish and go home.

As I ran, I took out a small alarm which I had in my pocket. It can make a loud sound to gain people's attention if I pull off a ring. I could see a woman pushing a child in a pushchair walking towards me and I felt a bit afraid, but I kept on running. Then I looked quickly over out of the corner of my eye to see the Asian man naked and whacking his penis!

I was shocked, but I kept on running. When I got home I was walking around the house, unsure of what to do next. I decided not to get in touch with the police as I did not want to be kept waiting for hours and the thought of trying to communicate with them with their lack of understanding put me off. But I did not sleep for a week.

Jamie and his then girlfriend Jenna came to visit me and I told him what had happened at the park. Jenna, who worked at the police station, said I should have reported it to the police straight away, and she said she would mention it when she went back to work. I did get text message that they wanted to interview me, but I waited and waited and it never happened.

One night I came home from work to find my house had been burgled. It wasn't the first time. It was the most horrible feeling in the world. The place was upside down and all our clothes were on the floor and all the drawers were open. Philip's computer games had been stolen and so had my jewels and money.

I did not want to call the police as I have no faith in them, but Philip was clearly upset. He called Jamie and my sister and they came to the house. We waited for three hours for the police and when they arrived I felt as if I was invisible to them. Again I got the 'never seen a deaf person before' look. I found them extremely unhelpful and so ignorant because they did not even ask me any questions. It was my house, and I was so upset.

One of the officers eventually asked me if I wanted to go to a victim support group, but I could not understand him. Jenna explained it to me about the victim support group and asked if an interpreter would help. It would have helped if they had known how to arrange the support and help I needed.

Philip was later asked to go to the police station to make a statement, but they never asked me to go. They asked Philip if I was blind! Nothing came out of it.

Another time I had problems with the police was when Philip was 18 and working at Marks & Spencers part time while he was at college. He was asked to fetch an M&S trolley from a nearby field near the fire station, and when he got to the field to pick up the trolley he was confronted by a drug dealer demanding money, and threatened with a knife and a syringe supposed to be full of Aids-infected blood. He did not have any money, so he ran as fast as he could, although he found it difficult to run because of his asthma. He managed to get to a house and asked the a man to call the police. This was around 4 pm. When he came home he was upset and went straight upstairs.

We didn't see the police till midnight, and again they were very unhelpful and giving me the 'never seen a deaf person before' look. I didn't feel comfortable wearing my dressing grown and I wanted to support my son, for he had had a distressing and traumatic experience. Philip had to wake me up nine hours later to ask me to make a statement, but I didn't want him to have to go through those experiences. I wanted to say a million things and deliver some angry words, but I couldn't. I had to stand up for my rights and for my son.

The police told my son that they thought they knew who the person was and said Philip was lucky, because it could have been much worse! I hoped and prayed it would never happen again and I would never have to ask for the police.

At The start of the credit crunch in 2008, Woolworths was the first shop to close and more were to follow. During the recession I started to worry about my job because the government were making cuts within the councils. The deaf centre was not affected at first, and but with so many benefits being cut it did not help the students and those who were receiving tax credits were also affected. Their benefit cuts meant students would not be able to attend the classes, which could affect my three classes. The council representatives promised to listen to us and they set up a meeting at the deaf centre which was packed with both deaf and hearing people, and the registered qualified interpreter was there.

The three council representatives listened to us as we stood up to get our points across. We all shared our concerns for our community. Then a reporter and photographer arrived from the local newspaper, surprising everyone. We were angry, as the Mayor did not attend or take any interest in coming to the deaf centre himself (although there were many photographs of him with deaf people upstairs in the conference room). They did not answer our questions, but the photographer took pictures and the journalist wrote down what we were saying.

The council representatives said they had taken everything into consideration and there would be more meetings. Further meetings did follow, and the final one was to be at the town hall. At the meeting the Mayor read out which buildings would be saved and which would have to close. Only a few of us attended, and we waited anxiously. The Mayor has a relative who is deaf and I was praying that the deaf centre would be saved, but it was on the list of those to be closed. One representative said it could be moved to a small building where the library used to be.

The following week we were allowed to go and see for ourselves, and it was obvious that a lot of work would be needed. After looking around I felt that the government had robbed our community of a nice building which was accessible. When it had opened in 1983, a lot of deaf people had given up their time to build it and decorate it to make it into a home for us. We had our own bar, where we could drink and chat on Friday evenings. The building had been refurbished about a year before the decision was made to close it. We had got a new roof on the main building and a new kitchen, car park and computer room for deaf people to take courses. There were toddler groups on Tuesday and Wednesday mornings and social workers would be there if any deaf people needed help. Pensioners could meet on Thursday afternoons for coffee and a chat or to play bingo.

A lot of money must have been spent on the building – I saw it myself as I was working there. It was a nice safe area, opposite the lovely park and easy accessible for deaf people who needed to use the bus. Where was I going to be working? I still had three classes and I was told that I would be moving elsewhere. But I did not have a car any more and working in the evenings most buses don't run after six o'clock. Luckily I still could work at the deaf centre one evening, but I could work at different places other evenings and I could get a lift on Monday evenings and still work at the deaf centre on Tuesday mornings and evenings.

When all the courses had finished for the summer, I would not return to work at the deaf centre again after working there for thirteen years, so I was sad to see it go. Returning after the summer break, I discovered that the council no longer offered yearly payment for my job but now only paid for the times I worked, and the payment for the students would be a lump sum payment, whereas previously it was monthly. This meant fewer people would be willing to pay all at once for the full course, and the government continued making more cuts. I then had to wait to see how many people would enrol. I was then given one class and less pay. And I was still attending the Job Centre.

What was I going to do now? I was still getting no help from the work programme or the Job Centre. My sister suggested I should work for myself, and found a company that helped people to set up their own businesses. We attended the first meeting and she explained the situation, and the lady said she would see if I could get off benefit and work with her till I could work for myself – brilliant, I thought. At the next meeting the lady called the Job Centre on my behalf, only to be told I could not receive help from her because I was on a work programmed. She said she would be happy to help me in her own time, for which I was very grateful. I went to see her on my own and had to write everything down on paper as they could not provide an interpreter. I found it difficult, but I was determined to try, and looked forward to working for myself and not having to attend the Job Centre any more.

As the weeks progressed the lady asked if I could borrow some money from a member of my family to help to fund my business. I asked my brother David, and he was more than happy to lend me the money. Once I had spent the money on some things I required I sent off the receipt, and when I received the funding money I was able to return the loan to my brother. I was hoping my business would be paid off, while I was still attending the Job Centre.

CHAPTER NINE

Looking back

My son Philip and his fiancée Beth, who I like very much, have been together now for five years and I am the grandmother of two beautiful grandsons, Archie, aged three, and Ben, two weeks old as I write this. When Archie was one and half years old Philip and Beth wanted me to babysit and I said I would love to but could not because of my deafness. 'I have an idea' said Beth, 'here is the baby monitor. If Archie cries, the colour on the monitor goes from green to red.' I said I could put it near the television and keep an eye on it. Good idea so I did babysit for the first time, but I have to confess I kept going upstairs to check! The monitor works and I have babysat a few times since.

My job involves teaching British Sign Language. I teach level one basic signs, which the student has to learn to finger spell, greetings, locations, family, buildings, food and drink, work. Slowly the student learns how to communicate with basic signs. Some learners do it for jobs or new skills, others for family reasons. If they pass the first level they can go on to do level two.

I remember a lady who wanted to learn because her

grandson was deaf. I asked her about her job and she told me she was manager for a delivery firm employing staff on computers. I asked her what she would do if a deaf person applied for a job in their office and she said 'absolutely not!' Yet she was attending the classes to learn to communicate with her grandson. British Sign Language is not a language you can learn in 30 weeks. It takes many years to become proficient and accurate.

British Sign Language is used by more than 70,000 deaf people in the UK, and it's the preferred language of the deaf community. It is a language in its own right with its own vocabulary and structure of grammar, expressed through movement of hands, body, face and head. Not every English word has a corresponding sign in BSL, so the interpreting process involves using a different vocabulary and grammatical structure. Like two-thirds of the world's languages it has no written form, but it is just as valued as any spoken/written language.

Here is another example of how ignorant people are with me, even with simple matters. As I get older I find reading more difficult and I thought I had better have my eyes tested. Philip came with me and we went into a very dark room, so I could not see when I was being told to move my eyes to the left or right. My son explained and the optician agreed to leave the door a little ajar. All went well and he was very helpful and patient. He gave me a card and told me to return next week to pick up the glasses. A week later I went to pick them up and I gave the young lady the card and I said I was deaf. She gave me the 'never met a deaf person before' look and walked away to speak to another woman. She gave the other lady my card and said she didn't want to serve her because she was scared, could she do it instead!

Philip's story

My mother asked me to put my thoughts into words about growing up with a deaf mother, but I wasn't sure why. I didn't have a bad childhood and I don't feel I was held back by my mother's disability, I've never felt she was a hindrance to me. I suppose that's why it is useful to put my thoughts into words, because of what a great job she did with us, especially on her own.

In primary school, I felt that my school mates had respect for my mother and her deafness. I was never taunted or bullied about her; in fact, they seemed to treat me better for it. That's how I felt anyway. On the odd occasion when my friends would be invited round, I would introduce them to my mother and they would try their best to communicate.

My mother has given me some questions that she wanted to me to answer here, but I found them confusing. I will try to explain. Mam asked me how much of a pain it was that I couldn't shout to her from upstairs while she was downstairs. She asked how much of a burden it was to have to help her communicate with other people when we were shopping or she needed something. She also asked me how much it bothered me that my friends' parents could hear and mine couldn't. But I never knew anything else. I had nothing to compare it to. This is why I've never felt that I've been at a disadvantage in any situation.

Since Mam told me she was writing this book, I've reflected on my childhood and things have slowly fallen into place. For example, when Jamie and I played with our friends outside, Mam would want us to stay close to the house, but my friends could go and play in other streets. We were never allowed to play outside when it was dark, yet my friends could play on the front. If we ever wandered off, Mam would come and find us within minutes and send us home. Now I completely understand why this was. Mam couldn't hear us playing outside, so she needed to be able to see us at all times.

I do have one particular memory that really sticks in my mind about growing up with a single, deaf mother. Jamie and I were about 8-10 years old when a new family moved in over the road. One of their kids was called Peter. He was about 13 and really tall, so Jamie and I looked up to him (pardon the pun). He made friends with a lot of kids his own age, but my friends and his friends all hung around the same street.

One day, Peter and his friends were taking the mick out of me and Jamie. I can't remember what it was about, but we both came home quite upset. We told Mam what had happened and within seconds, her coat and shoes were on and she was out of the door looking for Peter. I remember looking out of the window and see her standing and shouting at him, which he and his friends thought was really funny. When Mam shouts, it doesn't sound like someone shouting, it's like a high-pitched scream. When she came home, she told us that she had told him off.

The next day, while we were out playing, Peter decided to have another go at us - again, I can't remember why. Jamie and I were upset again and came home, but we didn't want to tell Mam, as we knew she would go and find him again. We eventually told her because she knew something was up. She went out to find him again and she did. This time there were more of Peter's friends there, all laughing as Mam gave him what for. For Peter, this was a great way to take the mick out of someone and it was obvious that he taunted us so he and his friends could stand and laugh at her. It's the most painful memory of my childhood, because we were all powerless to do anything about it. He was surrounded by his friends and we were only small. I look back now and regret not trying to do more, but we were only kids and we were intimidated. Peter has probably forgotten that all this happened. It was over 20 years ago, but I still think about it now.

My father was never really good to us. Back then there were no mobile phones and texting, so there was no way that my parents could communicate other than face-to-face. Dad was supposed to have Jamie and me every Saturday and we couldn't wait to see him. Every weekend was like Christmas to us, and we loved being with him. Every Saturday from 12.30pm, Jamie and I would sit on the window sill looking out of the window, waiting for him to come. We would have our coats on and our shoes by the door so we could dash out as soon as he arrived.

I remember the first Saturday that he didn't turn up. We were sitting waiting for him and when he didn't arrive at 1 pm, we assumed he was running late and just waited longer. But by the time 2 pm came, we were deflated and upset because we knew he wouldn't be coming for us.

Mam could see that we were upset, so she would take us to the park and play games with us. She never said a bad word about him to us; she would just say that he must have been so busy he couldn't come.

The following week Jamie and I again had have our coats at the ready from 12.30 pm, unsure if he would turn up, but excited at the same time. This time he did turn up, but Mam told us to wait inside while she went outside to speak to him. We could hear her shouting at him, but we couldn't really understand what she was saying. All we wanted to do was to see him and go and play with him. We poked our hands through the letterbox to try and grab his hand while Mam was shouting at him. He was like a celebrity to us.

While I was trying to poke my hand through the letterbox, I was thinking 'Why won't my Mam let me see my Dad?' He only had us for four hours every Saturday and he didn't really take us places or anything, but we didn't care, we were with him. We obviously had no idea what was going on, but resentment against Mam was building every time she stopped us going outside while she shouted at him. We hadn't seen him for two or three weeks and now he was here and we still couldn't see him. Why?

Mam couldn't explain what he was really like, we were still kids. That must have been to awful, for her to watch us fall over each other to get to him, knowing what he had done in the past.

When I got to about 14, I wanted to be with my friends more. They would go to town on Saturdays, shopping. I started to go with them, which meant I wouldn't see my Dad, but Jamie would still go. I also started asking my Mam a lot of questions about my Dad. Questions like 'How long were you married for?', 'What was he like to live with?' and 'Why did you split up?' Mam couldn't lie to me, and all her answers led to more questions.

Over a period of a few months, I went from wanting to be with him all the time to not wanting to be with him at all. It got more and more obvious to me that picking us up every Saturday was more of a chore to him than a pleasure. Most of the time, we would just sit and watch TV. Jamie didn't know anything about the questions I'd been asking, but I did tell him that we shouldn't see him any more. Jamie didn't take much convincing, because he was bored with sitting and watching the TV for four hours every Saturday too.

Then one day, he came for us at 1 pm on a Saturday. We had written a note to him – I remember it saying 'We don't want to see you any more'. I was upstairs in my Mam's bedroom looking down at Dad's car and Jamie went to the car, opened the door, threw the note in, closed the door and came back into the house. I was crying so much. Dad then started beeping the horn, but he never got out. He stopped beeping the horn and revved the car and wheelspun away. Jamie and I were crying, but we knew it was the right thing to do. Things just hadn't been the same with him for a long time. I've always really wanted a father figure in my life, even to this day, but my dad had never really been a good example.

Mam never really had another partner because she was so focused on us. Throughout my teenage years, I got some help from my grandfather. He took me fishing and he also taught me how to shave. I once asked my uncle for some advice about girls too. That was really it.

I now have two boys of my own and I'm trying to be the best father I can be. In a way, I'm almost grateful to my father for being the way he was, because I feel that I know how to treat my kids better.

Jamie's story

My turn now! I asked Phil if we should combine these statements as I felt we would be pretty much saying the same thing, but when I read his bit I said straight away, 'let's do it separately'.

I really remember the daft things, like when we used to play out and Mam would shout at us if we went too far down the road and out of her view without telling her, but we would be embarrassed when she shouted, because as Phil said it's very different. On the other hand, if anyone said anything or took the mick then we would be very defensive! We would then have to ask her every time we went somewhere if it was OK first, as we didn't want the same embarrassing shouting to happen all the time, but also out of respect as well.

In school I didn't have any problems with having a deaf mother. Phil and I didn't need to learn sign language as we would pick it up off Mam all the time even though she didn't use it with us. However the school capitalized on this because they would make me get up in front of the whole class and teach them the 'I can sing a rainbow' song in sign language as we sang. It definitely has its positives, as I put on my CV that I can speak another language and whenever I encounter deaf people in my job I'm always the one that helps them as my colleagues run a mile!

Back to growing up. The only thing that bothered me was the luxuries my friends' parents could afford, as they had jobs. I felt it was difficult for us growing up and only being allowed to have one or the other of two treats, not both – for example if we went to the shop for a treat we couldn't have crisps, chocolate and a drink, it was one only. Takeaways were very infrequent too. We had to save up to be poor - I'm joking when I say that, but it did feel sometimes like that.

I remember one year at school around Christmas time we had to bring in daft stuff like cans of fruit, boxes of chocolates, biscuits, that sort of thing for a hamper that was going to a family that was underprivileged. This box was HUGE and full of nice expensive food. I was happy that I was helping a less fortunate family out at Christmas. Some people (those with rich parents) brought presents in like cars, or dolls depending on the family we were providing for. I was so grateful that we weren't as hard up as that family.

A few days later we were all at home and there was a knock at the door. I opened it first, then Mam came and Phil. I couldn't believe my eyes - it was a man and a kid with a massive hamper full of all these things I have just mentioned, but from a different school. I felt so disappointed that we were now classed as the underprivileged ones. I was also grateful, don't get me wrong, but I thought there must be a mistake! My Mam's face lit up, and she was almost tearful. Phil was over the moon too, but I just took a step back thinking I didn't want anything. I didn't dare tell any of my friends!

They all had their own bedrooms, but Phil and I had to share. All these things got me down at a very young age but I thought there was nothing I can do about it, I was just a kid. From those days I never asked for help with anything. I just knew when I grew older that I wanted to provide for my family and work hard for my money. My brother will say I'm tight, but I'd like to think I grew up with nothing and I still have most of it!

The next year we did the same thing with the hamper again and I was scared in case the family they were talking about was mine again, but it wasn't, we only got it once.

I have the same story as Phil with my friends meeting Mam, but to me talking to my Mam is no different from talking with you. I've grown up with the way Mam talks all my life, so I can understand everything she says, and Mam just lip reads everything I say, so there's no boundaries. I did feel unhappy that I couldn't just shout down to my Mam from up the stairs when all my mates could, or when mobiles came out and my friends and their parents would ring each other but I couldn't do that. We did have a house phone and if it rang Phil or I would run down the stairs to answer it (that's if it didn't stop, I'm sure people would do it on purpose) and usually it would be my Nana wanting to organise something with Mam, so we would have to be the middle man. I have just recently made the first ever phone call to my Mam 15 years after the invention of mobile phones by Face Time, to you that may seem nothing, but I've never been able to do that before.

Michael (I'm not saying Dad because he was never that to me or Phil) was the worst. He didn't know how to provide for his kids, and the less said about him the better in my opinion. I just remember kids at school saying where they had been at weekends (in cars, but we never had one) or where their dads took them, but my story was the same every week, I watched Mr Bean and went food shopping. (Mr Bean is brilliant, but that's not the point.) Michael would give us £1 pocket money each almost every week, but he would spend £20 on the lottery. We were old enough not to be bothered about how much we got every week, but we wanted to ask why we got so little just out of principle, so we sat Michael and his girlfriend down and asked them why and they said they couldn't afford it. When we mentioned the £20 they put on the lottery every week they just made an excuse, trying to shut us up. We weren't bothered really, but it made me and Phil closer, as we really knew what was going on. I guess that's what made me grow up so quickly, knowing the value of money and respecting how much hard work Mam had put into looking after us both. Shortly after we stopped seeing Michael Mam started giving us more pocket money a week and I started saving up for daft stuff like magazines or clothes.

Now I see how much of a great father Phil is to my nephews and I love watching him spoil them. I love spoiling them too, as it makes you appreciate them more when you give them that little bit more attention.

I definitely approved of Mam's idea to write this book, as the world needs to understand that not all people with disabilities can just crack on with life when they don't get the help. An obese person can claim disability allowance and get a free car because they are obese. All this help from the government because they can't work as a result of being fat? My Mam desperately wants a job, but because she's deaf she can't do half the jobs the obese person can. They take advantage of the their disability and simply WON'T get a job! As you can tell this frustrates me, as I can only help my mam so much, as I have a job, a mortgage and bills to pay, otherwise all the family would help her 24/7.

But back to the question of how growing up with a deaf

parent was for me. It was what it was. I believe in living in the moment. I can't change the past, as it's been and gone. The now is what's happening and the future isn't here yet, but I know I will make sure my future and my children's future will be the best I can make it. It hasn't been a sad childhood by any means, just slightly different. Phil and I would make it as normal as we could, and by normal I mean like the childhood of everyone else who didn't encounter the difficulties we faced with various things.

Phil and I could write forever, but this isn't about us, so we hope this is enough for you to understand a little bit about what it was for us to have a deaf mother.

We love you Mam and we know that this book will touch people's hearts in the right places and hopefully change people's perception of the deaf and start to fix things that are wrong with the way society treats the deaf community over jobs.

In conclusion

In writing this book, my computer has helped to some extent with the grammar and spelling, but I still need help with it. I would say to myself while I was typing, 'My deafness is not going to hold me back - I can write this book about my life and I am going to do it'.

There are some terrible cases, much worse than mine. Back in 1929, Mattie Hope was institutionalized in the Forest Haven Home for the Retarded for 57 years until it was discovered she was deaf. Hope had not been tested appropriately, and that was the reason for her misdiagnosis.

In another case in 1984, a man in New York was put into a home and he spent almost ten years in homes for the retarded. There was a law suit over his case.

In Tulsa, Oklahoma, a boy of 17 who had spent 12 years in a school for the retarded was found to be deaf.

The Beacon Journal (Akron, Ohio) reported on 30 May 2002 the story of a 48-year-old deaf man who had spent the first 18 years of his life in a home for the retarded after doctors advised his parents to institutionalize him.

Imagine you go to McDonald's to order breakfast to take it to work. The menu is in English, but the staff can only understand Greek.

Imagine you accidentally fall on some stairs at work and injure your arm. Your colleagues take you to hospital, but the doctor and nurses treating you are speaking in Swahili.

Imagine going to college for the first night of a course to learn art, only to find the teacher can only speak Polish?

Imagine wanting to compliment the chef for an excellent meal in an Italian restaurant, and finding that he doesn't know a single word of English.

Be honest with yourself. Are you at home right now? Switch on your television and turn off the volume for ten minutes and keep watching…

Famous deaf people, and champions of the deaf

Charlie Chaplin (1889-1977) was actor, director, producer, and composer. The clown from Lambeth was influenced by many deaf actors he worked with in his silent films. In that era deaf and hearing audiences enjoyed the same level of participation, and Chaplin would enthrall his entire audiences with his facial expressions, posture, touch and movement. Chaplin made friends with Granville Redmond, who had become deaf at the age of two and half years from scarlet fever. He never learned to speak and Charlie Chaplin became a friend and a collector of Granville's artwork. Charlie learned sign language and finger spelling and was given credit for influencing Chaplin's acting. Chaplin did not move his lips in his silent films. He used gestures and expressions resembling those used by deaf persons. Granville took some minor roles in a few of Chaplin's films.

Prince Philip's mother was deaf and he used to learn to lip read with his mother, though I don't think he used British Sign Language.

Helen Keller was the first deaf and blind person to earn a Bachelor of Arts degree. She was well-travelled and outspoken in her convictions and communicated with others as conventionally as possible. She learned to speak and spent much of her life giving speeches and lectures. She learned to use her hand on people's lips with her hands and she had a sense of touch which became extremely subtle. She became proficient at using Braille and reading sign language with her hands as well. Through her life she used companions to help her.

The deaf American Oscar-winning actress Marlee Matlin, who starred with William Hurt in the film 'Children of a Lesser God', used American Sign Language, and there were many other deaf people in that film, which was about a love affair with a teacher. She continues to make films and programmes, and there are other deaf actresses in America today.

Princess Diana herself learned how to use British Sign Language, and at the British Deaf Association centenary congress she made a faultless speech using it. The 800 delegates were delighted and gave her a standing ovation. She had been learning to sign for seven years in her role as patron to this association. She was taught by a deaf teacher and was excellent.

The BBC's CBeebies children's programmes with four young people feature poetry for children translated with British Sign Language. It's a wonderful programme for both deaf and hearing children.

Every day on the BBC news channel 24, from one o'clock to half past one, there is a registered qualified level six British Sign Language interpreter.